D1109451

A GIFT FOR

....

FROM

....

DATE

....

THE

MIRACLE

OF

PEACE

*You Can Find Peace in
Every Challenge You Face*

JACK COUNTRYMAN

COUNTRYMAN®

An Imprint of Thomas Nelson Publishers

THOMAS NELSON
Since 1798

The Miracle of Peace
© 2022 Jack Countryman

All rights reserved. No portion of this book may be reproduced, stored in a retrieval system, or transmitted in any form or by any means— electronic, mechanical, photocopy, recording, scanning, or other—except for brief quotations in critical reviews or articles, without the prior written permission of the publisher.

Published in Nashville, Tennessee, by Thomas Nelson. Thomas Nelson is a registered trademark of HarperCollins Christian Publishing, Inc.

Thomas Nelson titles may be purchased in bulk for educational, business, fund-raising, or sales promotional use. For information, please email SpecialMarkets@ThomasNelson.com.

Unless otherwise noted, Scripture quotations are from the New King James Version*. Copyright © 1982 by Thomas Nelson. Used by permission. All rights reserved. Scripture quotations marked AMP are from the Amplified* Bible (AMP). Copyright © 2015 by The Lockman Foundation. Used by permission. www.Lockman.org. Scripture quotations marked KJV are from the King James Version. Public domain. Scripture quotations marked MSG are from THE MESSAGE. Copyright © 1993, 2002, 2018 by Eugene H. Peterson. Used by permission of NavPress. All rights reserved. Represented by Tyndale House Publishers, a Division of Tyndale House Ministries. Scripture quotations marked NASB are from the New American Standard Bible* (NASB). Copyright © 1960, 1962, 1963, 1968, 1971, 1972, 1973, 1975, 1977, 1995, 2020 by The Lockman Foundation. Used by permission. www.Lockman.org. Scripture quotations marked NLT are from the Holy Bible, New Living Translation. Copyright © 1996, 2004, 2015 by Tyndale House Foundation. Used by permission of Tyndale House Ministries, Carol Stream, Illinois 60188. All rights reserved. Scripture quotations marked NRSV are from the New Revised Standard Version Bible. Copyright © 1989 National Council of the Churches of Christ in the United States of America. Used by permission. All rights reserved worldwide.

Cover design by Ingrid Pakats, Shutterstock
Interior design by Kristy L. Edwards

ISBN 978-1-4002-3839-2 (Audiobook)
ISBN 978-1-4002-3553-7 (eBook)
ISBN 978-1-4002-3552-0 (HC)

Printed in China

22 23 24 25 GRI 10 9 8 7 6 5 4 3 2 1

CONTENTS

INTRODUCTION

When I was in my forties, I was struggling to succeed in the business world. I wanted to accomplish more than just making a living; I wanted to do well in my career. At the same time, I was in a men's Bible study. One morning our focus was Philippians 4:6–7: "Be anxious for nothing, but in everything by prayer and supplication, with thanksgiving, let your requests be made known to God; and the peace of God, which surpasses all understanding, will guard your hearts and minds through Christ Jesus."

Those verses spoke directly to me—and changed my life. That morning I claimed those verses for myself and made a choice to cease worrying about whether or not I would succeed in business and life. I chose to let God direct my life, as well as my marriage, and to be at peace with my relationship with my heavenly Father.

As I look back on the forty-seven years since that life-changing morning, I can truly say based on my own life that the peace of God is an indescribable, unfathomable gift. Just as I and other Christians I know have experienced, you can know God's great blessing of His peace that passes all understanding. As we journey through life, God truly wants us to be at peace with Him, with other people, and with ourselves. We come to know the peace of God when, first, we recognize our sin, receive His forgiveness, and name His Son, Jesus, as our Savior and Lord. Then we put God first in our lives: we let Him guide everything we say and do; we go to Him for guidance; and we trust the promises we find in His Word. There is no other path to finding peace with God.

In fact, whenever I try to live without Jesus as my Shepherd and King, I've found myself lost and helpless. But when I have Christ at the center of my life, I find that He enables me to do all the things He calls me to do and that He blesses me each day with His peace. My prayer is that this book will help you know God better and therefore experience His peace more fully—and may His peace serve as a constant reminder of His everlasting love for you.

JACK COUNTRYMAN

Some of the sons of Benjamin and Judah came to David at the stronghold. And David went out to meet them, and answered and said to them, "If you have come peaceably to me to help me, my heart will be united with you; but if to betray me to my enemies, since there is no wrong in my hands, may the God of our fathers look and bring judgment." Then the Spirit came upon Amasai, chief of the captains, and he said:

"We are yours, O David;
We are on your side, O son of Jesse!
Peace, peace to you,
And peace to your helpers!
For your God helps you."

So David received them, and made them captains of the troop.

1 CHRONICLES 12:16–18

1

CHOOSING PEACE
WITH EACH OTHER

We've all had the experience of being in a conversation that gets more and more intense, and we reach a point when we aren't sure which way the conversation will go. Emotions encourage us to win the argument or return an insult for an insult. What if, instead, we chose to make peace with that brother or sister in Christ?

God's way is the way of peace. He also wants unity among His followers. When—by His grace—we get past how we feel and seek to be at peace with our brothers and sisters, we can experience a change of heart and possibly avoid saying or doing something we will regret in the future. So take to God in prayer whatever aspect of the conversation—or the person!—is bothering you. Listen for the Holy Spirit to be your guide and rely on Him to enable you to obey.

To settle or to avoid a conflict, first turn to God and seek His Spirit's guidance. God is always ready for us to come to Him with an open heart and mind. He is always ready to provide you with the wisdom you need (James 1:5).

REFLECTION

If you were to stop and listen for God the next time conflict arises, what might you expect to hear from Him?

Grace to you and peace [inner calm and spiritual well-being] from God our Father and the Lord Jesus Christ.

1 CORINTHIANS 1:3 AMP

2

PEACE FROM ABOVE

Three years ago—and one month after I had fallen and hit the side of my face—my wife, Marsha, and I were watching television. When I turned to her to speak, I couldn't utter a single word. When we called the doctor the next morning, the nurse told me to go to the local medical center immediately—and we did.

Discovering that I had blood on the brain, the doctor sent me to Vanderbilt, where I learned that I had three options: (1) wait and see if the blood was absorbed into my body; (2) have a craniotomy where they remove a portion of my skull and stop the bleeding; or (3) have a burr hole surgery where they drill one or more small holes in my head and use a tube to drain off the blood. Without hesitation, I decided to have the burr hole surgery. What amazes me is that I had no doubt or fear; I was completely at peace. Later, when I went into the hospital for the surgery, I had the same confidence that God was in charge and He would take care of me. And He did.

Two weeks after the surgery, I went to see my family doctor. He looked me in the eyes and asked, "Jack, do you know how lucky you are? Seven out of ten people die when they have blood on the brain."

As I think back on that entire situation, I realize I never feared for my life. Every step of the way, God gave me a sense of peace that I cannot explain. I had no doubt that He was with me and that I would come through the surgery just fine.

When you choose to turn your life over to God, the Holy Spirit within you becomes your Comforter (John 14:16 KJV). Praise God! What a blessing!

REFLECTION

Walk through—as I just did—a time in your life when you had to face fear head-on. Comment on the degree of peace you had or didn't have each step of the way.

THE ONE WHO WANTS TO ENJOY LIFE AND SEE
  GOOD DAYS *[good—whether apparent or
  not]*,
MUST KEEP HIS TONGUE FREE FROM EVIL
  AND HIS LIPS FROM SPEAKING GUILE
  (treachery, deceit).
HE MUST TURN AWAY FROM WICKEDNESS AND
  DO WHAT IS RIGHT.
HE MUST SEARCH FOR PEACE *[with God, with
  self, with others]* AND PURSUE IT EAGERLY
  [actively—not merely desiring it].
FOR THE EYES OF THE LORD ARE *[looking
  favorably]* UPON THE RIGHTEOUS *(the
  upright)*,
AND HIS EARS ARE ATTENTIVE TO THEIR
  PRAYER *(eager to answer)*,
BUT THE FACE OF THE LORD IS AGAINST THOSE
  WHO PRACTICE EVIL.

1 PETER 3:10–12 AMP

3

GOD WANTS TO BLESS YOU

I t's not just a celebration of Thanksgiving. Nor should it become rote and robotic. I'm talking about considering all that you have as a result of God's grace, all that you have to thank Him for; all that you have—period.

For starters, God may have given you good health, a job, and a place to live. Add five—or ten or twenty or more—items to your list. Then thank God for His love, His mercy, and His grace.

Next, consider what good it does to complain about what you don't have or about the current circumstances of your life. According to Scripture, "THE EYES OF THE LORD ARE . . . UPON THE RIGHTEOUS (the upright), AND HIS EARS ARE ATTENTIVE TO THEIR PRAYER" (1 Peter 3:12 AMP). What a wonderful promise—and invitation! Know that God hears your prayers; that He longs to bless your life; and that His peace is only one of the gifts He has for you. Draw near to God every waking moment of every single day, for in His presence you will be blessed to know His peace.

REFLECTION

Think about what keeps you from drawing near to God in the course of your day. Consider what may be keeping you from hearing His voice. Then determine how to remove, overcome, or avoid those obstacles.

Paul, Silvanus, and Timothy,

To the church of the Thessalonians in God the Father and the Lord Jesus Christ:

Grace to you and peace from God our Father and the Lord Jesus Christ.

We give thanks to God always for you all, making mention of you in our prayers, remembering without ceasing your work of faith, labor of love, and patience of hope in our Lord Jesus Christ. . . . For our gospel did not come to you in word only, but also in power, and in the Holy Spirit. . . .

And you became followers of us and of the Lord, having received the word in much affliction, with joy of the Holy Spirit.

1 THESSALONIANS 1:1–3, 5–6

4

PEACE WITH GOD

HANK HANEGRAAFF

This passage from 1 Thessalonians reminds me of my good friend Hank Hanegraaff. For four years, Hank faced a battle to overcome his fight with stage 4 mantle cell lymphoma cancer. I asked Hank about the peace God gave him during that trial.

When my dear friend Jack Countryman asked me to write on peace, I considered it a daunting task. Not because I have not experienced peace. Rather, because—as St. Paul explained—"The peace of God transcends all understanding."

The gospel of peace is a preview of the promise of perfect peace in paradise. In the present, our peace is yet unperfected. But as followers of the Lamb, we continue on toward the certain promise that one day we will step over the threshold of the Jordan into an eternal ocean of perfect peace. Thus, those who stand firm with their feet fitted with the readiness that comes from the gospel of peace are only a heartbeat away from perfect peace.

Through peace with God, peace with others, and the promise of certain peace in paradise, we are equipped to face all the trials and tribulations life brings our way. While I have contemplated such peace in previous writings, I have never experienced the ocean of God's peace half as much as I did when I lay in a hospital bed in full face of my own mortality. After I had already fought a four-year battle with stage 4 mantle cell lymphoma, tumors overwhelmed my physical body. The chance that I would survive began to look increasingly bleak. Yet, during the most agonizing part of the process, I can testify that God's peace was an existential reality. I was bathed in the ocean of His providential peace and rejoiced in His power and presence in the midst of my pain. Thus, I can wholeheartedly testify to a peace that I am at a loss to adequately explain.

REFLECTION

Describe a time when you experienced, if not "the ocean of God's peace," at least a few substantial waves.

Concerning brotherly love you have no need that I should write to you, for you yourselves are taught by God to love one another; and indeed you do so toward all the brethren who are in all Macedonia. But we urge you, brethren, that you increase more and more; that you also aspire to lead a quiet life, to mind your own business, and to work with your own hands, as we commanded you, that you may walk properly toward those who are outside, and that you may lack nothing.

1 THESSALONIANS 4:9–12

5

A BROTHER'S LOVE
AND GOD'S PEACE

When I think about my brothers in Christ, I am overcome with appreciation for their selfless and Christlike love and care for me. Through the years I have learned much from the ways they lead and the lives they model. These godly men have helped me live a peaceful life, and through their friendships God showers me with His love, His joy, and His peace.

These brothers in Christ have also encouraged me by their words and their example to seek God in everything I say and do. So my prayer each day is for God to be at the center of my life, and I ask Him to "let the words of my mouth and the meditation of my heart be acceptable in Your sight, O Lord, my strength and my Redeemer" (Psalm 19:14). The result is a lifestyle that honors and pleases God.

This lifestyle is also a winsome witness to the world. After all, God calls all who have chosen to follow Jesus to be His witness in this lost world. When we live so that others may see Christ in us, God uses us to shine the light of His love and truth. People we come in contact with just may ask us what makes us different, and then we can tell them what Jesus means to us.

REFLECTION

One thoughtful and anonymous believer once asked, "If you were arrested for being a Christian, would there be enough evidence in your life to convict you?" What evidence would you point to? (A friend might be able to help you.) What might you do to ensure the presence of stronger evidence? Be specific.

We urge you, brethren, to recognize those who labor among you, and are over you in the Lord and admonish you, and to esteem them very highly in love for their work's sake. Be at peace among yourselves.

1 THESSALONIANS 5:12–13

6

LIVING AT PEACE WITH YOUR BROTHERS AND SISTERS

I t can be difficult to live at peace with others at times, whether it be coworkers, family members, neighbors, friends, or really anyone we cross paths with regularly. Personalities, politics, passions, practices, values and goals, ideas and beliefs—all of these and more can become reasons for conflict. However, when we reach out to people with God's love, conflict can melt away. When we "comfort the fainthearted, uphold the weak, [are] patient with all" (1 Thessalonians 5:14), we improve the chances that we will live at peace with the people we encounter. Such behaviors are learned (what an encouraging truth!), and they also bring glory to God.

Now, I know the list of all that can spark conflict is long, but don't be discouraged. I have learned in my ninety-one years that the closer I walk with God, the less I am bothered with the way other people act. The greater attention I give to God's presence with me, the more I experience His love, mercy, and grace in an abundance that enables me to share His love, mercy, and grace with others—and that is great conflict prevention. Also, when I make my relationship with my heavenly Father the top priority in my life, I cope better with the inevitable rough patches of relationships with people. In fact, the more completely I lean on my God, the more I experience His peace that passes all understanding. Try it!

REFLECTION

Explain your thoughts about why being at peace with God improves our relationships with fellow human beings, especially fellow Christ-followers.

Now may the God of peace Himself sanctify you through and through [that is, separate you from profane and vulgar things, make you pure and whole and undamaged—consecrated to Him—set apart for His purpose]; and may your spirit and soul and body be kept complete and [be found] blameless at the coming of our Lord Jesus Christ. Faithful and absolutely trustworthy is He who is calling you [to Himself for your salvation], and He will do it [He will fulfill His call by making you holy, guarding you, watching over you, and protecting you as His own].

1 THESSALONIANS 5:23–24 AMP

7

PEACE WITH GOD

O. S. HAWKINS

O. S. Hawkins is an author and friend, and I had the privilege of publishing his ten most recent books. His humor is contagious, and we banter back and forth about life and its many challenges. To say I am fortunate to have a friend like O. S. is an understatement.

There is something special about the firstborn child. We find this truth laced all through the Bible and know it to be true in our own experiences. Who of us can forget the birth of our first child? Yes, the birth of the firstborn child is special, as is the birth of the firstborn grandchild.

Jackson Hawkins Shivers entered our world on January 18, 2003. From the moment I first held him, I knew that this namesake of mine and I were going to have a special relationship. It began at that moment and has grown stronger across the years.

When Jackson was three years old, his parents were on a trip to California, and my wife and I had the joy of keeping him all to ourselves for a few days. Sitting in my lap at my office, he pointed and asked me, "Poppy, what is that?" I replied, "A letter opener" and let him hold it. The next thing I knew, with a jerk of his arm, that letter opener was sticking in his left eye. He went through several surgeries during the weeks following, and the weight of knowing it was all my fault robbed me of sleep, peace, and just about anything else for those many days and weeks. When Jackson was older, surgeons were able to sew onto his eye an intraocular lens, and today—by God's grace—he sees perfectly without any sign of past trauma. The experience brought our family to a new level of dependence upon God and of trusting in His will that we had never known before.

Peace came . . . eventually. It always comes to those who hold to God's promises. But those early weeks after the incident with the letter opener were like a laceration on my arm trying to heal. The healing process goes well until you bump something and the wound opens back up. After a while even a deep heart wound does in fact heal . . . although often the scars of an experience remain and remind.

As I write this, Jackson is a six-foot-five basketball

standout in his last year of high school and about to head off to college. Looking back at the journey we traveled together when he was so young, we understand Romans 8:28. We know—as only members of God's forever family know—that, yes, "all things work together for good to those who love God, to those who are the called according to His purpose."

REFLECTION

When we find it difficult to not blame ourselves for certain circumstances or a specific event, what can we ask of God so that we can experience His comfort and peace?

Grace to you and peace [inner calm and spiritual well-being] from God our Father and the Lord Jesus Christ.

Blessed [gratefully praised and adored] be the God and Father of our Lord Jesus Christ, the Father of mercies and the God of all comfort, who comforts and encourages us in every trouble so that we will be able to comfort and encourage those who are in any kind of trouble, with the comfort with which we ourselves are comforted by God. For just as Christ's sufferings are ours in abundance [as they overflow to His followers], so also our comfort [our reassurance, our encouragement, our consolation] is abundant through Christ [it is truly more than enough to endure what we must].

2 CORINTHIANS 1:2–5 AMP

8

KNOWING GOD'S COMFORT AND PEACE

T hink about a time when—if ever—life was hard, you were struggling, you prayed with not much more than a mustard seed of faith, and the situation got worse instead of better.

One time I was in business with a man I found difficult to get along with, and I wanted a change. Yet the harder I worked to improve our relationship, nothing changed . . . until, as I prayed, I finally released the situation to God. Oh, I kept working hard, but I let go of the relationship; I stepped out of the way to let God do whatever He was going to do. I stayed faithful to the task I knew I had to do. I stopped worrying about the outcome, and God blessed me with a certain sense of comfort and peace.

It was amazing how God turned our business around, and ten months later we sold the company to Thomas Nelson. During the twenty-five years between that sale and now, God has blessed us beyond our wildest imagination. Our good God loves to give good gifts to His children, and He grows our faith as we wait.

REFLECTION

List a handful of things that keep you from trusting God—and then what you will do to overcome each one of those.

Trust in the LORD with all your heart,
And lean not on your own understanding;
In all your ways acknowledge Him,
And He shall direct your paths.

PROVERBS 3:5-6

9

THE COMFORT OF GOD'S PEACE

SCOTT LEHMAN

Twenty-three years ago I met Scott Lehman. He and his wife, Leslie, came to JCountryman hoping to get permission to use the phrase "In His Grip" for a ministry he wanted to start. We had published a book by that title, and that book had influenced Scott to become a Christian. During our meeting, I was touched by his humble sincerity, and I offered to become his spiritual mentor, a role that has continued to this day. In His Grip is a golf ministry with one mission: to lead men to Jesus Christ through the game of golf. I recently talked to Scott about a time when he experienced the peace of God.

One of my favorite places on earth is Priest Lake, Idaho. I have been going there with my wife's family for over twenty years. It is a place where God refreshes and restores my soul. To me, Priest Lake is where heaven comes down to earth.

Back in July 2017, we again found ourselves embarking on a week's family vacation at Priest Lake. It had been an unusual year. As founder and president of In His Grip ministry since 2007, I had been struggling for several months as to the organization's future. Local churches had been forced to reduce their financial support of the ministry, a reality that forced me into a season of hard, fervent prayer and constantly seeking the Lord's guidance and direction. Yet all I heard was crickets. Frustration and anxiety were setting in; I found peace nowhere.

Then, early one morning, I found myself sitting at the end of the dock crying out to God, asking Him why He was so silent and pleading for His guidance. Tears were streaming down my face, and as one hit the surface of the lake, I experienced the voice of the Lord speaking into the depths of my soul.

God said, "My son, as you look out over the stillness of these waters, you fail to realize that I am working in the depths of your heart and soul to prepare you for where I am taking you. I never rest; I am always at work preparing the way for you. Be patient, My son. Keep seeking Me and crying out to Me. I hear your every word, and I catch in the palm of My hand every tear you shed. Remember, too, that My timing is never early, and it is never late. My timing is always perfect—as you will soon realize."

I was overwhelmed by the Lord's presence with me, and when I lifted my head, I felt a peace that truly transcended all understanding. I absolutely knew that God was with me. I also realized that I needed to continue to remember and live out my life verse. To be specific, I needed to trust in the Lord with all my heart and lean not on my own understanding. Instead, I needed, in all my ways, to acknowledge Him as Lord and to trust that He will make my path straight.

REFLECTION

When did you least understand what God was doing in your life? To what degree did you have peace at that time? Identify the factors that may have contributed to the presence or absence of peace.

Show Your marvelous lovingkindness by Your
     right hand,
O You who save those who trust in You
From those who rise up against them.
Keep me as the apple of Your eye;
Hide me under the shadow of Your wings,
From the wicked who oppress me,
From my deadly enemies who surround me.

PSALM 17:7–9

10

GOD'S PROTECTION

MARSHA COUNTRYMAN

I have been married to my lovely wife, Marsha, for fifty-five years. During that time our love for each other has grown, and I appreciate her more today than ever. I have asked her to share about a time many years ago when she experienced God's protection and His peace.

Many years ago when I was only nineteen years old, I was driving home from the children's studio where I taught dance. I stopped at a stop sign and turned left. That was all I remembered when I woke up in an ambulance and a firefighter was asking me questions. I was feeling intense pain in my right leg, but I kept my eyes closed. I didn't see—I didn't want to see—what was going on, but I heard the men talking.

When I asked what had happened and why my leg hurt, he just said he had to put a wrap on my leg because I had been in a wreck. I told him to save my blood if there was bleeding because I was anemic. He chuckled and said he'd do that. Throughout the ride in the ambulance, I felt the peace of God: I knew I was in the capable hands of not only the firefighters but also my Lord.

The next thing I remember was waking up in a hospital bed. A sheet draped over an aluminum frame covered my lower body, but nothing was touching me. Having no idea of the extent of my injury, I started asking questions.

I learned that a lumber truck had been speeding when his brakes locked. He hit my driver's side, and— seatbelt laws were not on the books at that time—I was thrown onto the street and in front of his locked wheels. I had rolled my long hair in huge plastic rollers because I had a date that night. Those rollers kept me from having my head bashed in, but I still got two black eyes. My right leg suffered the greatest amount of damage. Skin grafting was taken from my left thigh to try to piece my leg together, but the surgeon said it didn't work too well since so much of my muscle had been torn away when I went sliding on the asphalt. I stayed in the hospital for three months, and the doctors used some special baths to help with healing. In the mornings some type of oil was mixed into the water, and in the evenings vinegar was added instead. I laughed when the nurses would say that I smelled like a salad.

I didn't experience any fear when I was in the hospital because I felt God's peace covering me. I just took one day at a time—and didn't look in a mirror until I had been there for about a month. I wasn't scared and I hadn't really cried until the day my surgeon came to discuss my situation. He explained that he was happy with how my leg was coming along and admitted that at one time he thought he might need to amputate my leg from the knee down if the site of the injury became infected! I started crying at those words! When he asked why I was crying when I hadn't cried before, I explained that I hadn't known just how bad off I was. The doctor was very kind and gave me a hug. He told me not to worry and reassured me that I was going to be okay.

I was able to start exercising slowly and had to walk with a stiff right leg for many weeks so I wouldn't damage my healing knee. As time went on, I started taking special ballet lessons to lengthen and strengthen my calf muscle.

Today, I sometimes forget which leg was damaged. And when someone asks me about my scar, I say, "I am so glad you asked. Let me tell you how God protected me in a car accident."

REFLECTION

We give God glory when we tell of His good deeds on behalf of His people. What example of His protecting you will you share this week—and with whom?

"Blessed are the peacemakers,
For they shall be called sons of God.
Blessed are those who are persecuted for
*   righteousness' sake,*
For theirs is the kingdom of heaven.
Blessed are you when they revile and persecute
*   you, and say all kinds of evil against*
*   you falsely for My sake. Rejoice and be*
*   exceedingly glad, for great is your reward*
*   in heaven, for so they persecuted the*
*   prophets who were before you."*

MATTHEW 5:9–12

11

PEACE WITH FRIENDS IN JESUS

JOEY HICKMAN

Through the In His Grip ministry, Joey Hickman has become one of my best friends. He is a genuine person who loves the Lord, he is transparent about his love for Christ, and he has experienced God's peace.

I stared in disbelief . . .

The bridge over the Hatchie River had collapsed minutes earlier, the river had claimed five vehicles, and eight motorists had died. And this was the moment when I was confronted with the sin in my life as well as my own mortality. God spoke clearly to me on the night of April 1, 1989. Images still play out in my head. On that bridge that night, I gave my life to Christ; I put my trust in Him as my Lord and my Savior.

At the time I was serving as a volunteer firefighter

in the Henning, Tennessee, fire department. At approximately 8:30 p.m. each of us received a call to report to the Hatchie River bridge—and to be prepared to stay for a while. I loaded up my gear and traveled the three miles from my house. When I arrived, I realized the catastrophic collapse had happened only minutes before.

One week earlier, I'd decided to quit drinking alcohol. I was twenty-six, I had a drinking problem, and my life was spinning out of control. That first week was hard, and I barely made it through those seven days without drinking. The night the bridge collapsed, I was home in front of the TV trying to stay away from alcohol. Every minute of trying by my own power to stay sober was hard.

At the bridge that night, I realized God was waiting on me to give Him control of my life. When I decided to yield to Him, the peace that passes all understanding came into my life. I was no longer trying to remain sober just to be sober. Now my life had purpose, and I no longer felt like I was about to spin out of control. For almost thirty-two years now, I have remained sober because of God's power and His grace. I never even had to go through a program or follow a detox plan. My life changed the instant I realized what my eternity would have been if I had been a victim of that bridge collapse.

Today, I am happily married with two children and a full life in Christ. My twenty-three-year-old daughter Shelby has severe special needs, and my wife, Susan, and I serve as her caregivers. It is God's peace that allows us to face the difficulties of this new role in our lives. When her health struggles weigh heavily on us, we rely on His strength to get us through. Had it not been for that night on that bridge where God met me, I don't know if I would be able to face each day of caring for Shelby. But His grace, His strength, and His peace enable me to serve in the caregiver role He has given me.

God waits for us to surrender ourselves to Him and accept His Son, Jesus, as our Lord and Savior. Once we do, we can all live in the center of His good and perfect will as we let Jesus live in us and work through us.

REFLECTION

Not every believer has a come-to-Jesus moment, but you might. Share what that was for you, or at least what you might consider the closest approximation of one.

*Behold, the eye of the L*ORD *is on those who fear*
        Him,
On those who hope in His mercy,
To deliver their soul from death,
And to keep them alive in famine.
*Our soul waits for the L*ORD*;*
He is our help and our shield.

PSALM 33:18–20

12

OUR HELP AND OUR SHIELD

Last summer Marsha and I spent some time in Montana, one of our favorite places to be.

One day when I was driving home after playing golf with a good friend, a truck crossed the middle line and headed right toward me. Without thinking, I jerked off the two-lane road onto the shoulder, barely missing the truck.

Whenever I think about that experience, I can only thank God for His protection. His Holy Spirit caused me to react and, as a result, avoid being hit by the oncoming truck. And I continue to be amazed that I didn't feel even the slightest sense of fear in those life-threatening moments. God was taking care of me, He was protecting me, and I was secure in His presence with me. I truly had a sense of peace—*His* peace—during that entire brief but potentially terrifying experience. To God be the glory!

God truly fulfilled His promise of peace in my life on that unforgettable day in Montana. And He clearly protected me. As one of my favorite country songs proclaims, Jesus took the wheel. Almighty God was my help and my shield.

REFLECTION

We don't know what God—who never slumbers or sleeps—protects us from in the course of a day. At certain moments, though, we become very aware. When, if ever, have you experienced God's intervening in your life and protecting you from harm? Briefly describe the circumstances and your thoughts and emotions throughout.

"I am the good shepherd. . . . My sheep hear My voice, and I know them, and they follow Me. And I give them eternal life, and they shall never perish; neither shall anyone snatch them out of My hand. My Father, who has given them to Me, is greater than all; and no one is able to snatch them out of My Father's hand."

JOHN 10:11, 27–29

13

FOLLOWING THE SHEPHERD

Only one source of peace that passes all understanding exists, and that source is our infinitely loving, powerful, and good God.

Too often in life we try to handle everything on our own. We think to ourselves, *I can handle this. I don't need anyone's help.* And those are the thoughts of a fool.

God gives us freedom in this life. We can choose to follow Him and obey His biblical instructions. We can also choose to go our own way, and when we do, He waits patiently for us to realize the error of our ways. God wants to guide each one of us, His children, and show us how to live and what to do in whatever circumstances we face. God has promised to be our shepherd and to guide us in life. Will you let Him?

God knows exactly what you are facing today and every day. Remember, too, that His way for you is perfect and His plans for you are always in your best interest. Again, I want to challenge you to live with God as your guide. Study His Word for direction. Spend time in prayer—but don't do all the talking. Spend some of that time listening. Learn to sense His presence with you— learn to abide in Him—and you will see that He is indeed your good Shepherd.

REFLECTION

Think about a time when you clearly knew God's direction for you. Did you follow Him? Why or why not? What were the consequences?

"Blessed [joyful, nourished by God's goodness] are those who hunger and thirst for righteousness [those who actively seek right standing with God], for they will be [completely] satisfied. . . .

"Blessed [anticipating God's presence, spiritually mature] are the pure in heart [those with integrity, moral courage, and godly character], for they will see God. . . .

"Blessed [comforted by inner peace and God's love] are those who are persecuted for doing that which is morally right, for theirs is the kingdom of heaven [both now and forever].

"Blessed [morally courageous and spiritually alive with life-joy in God's goodness] are you when people insult you and persecute you, and falsely say all kinds of evil things against you because of [your association with] Me. Be glad and exceedingly joyful, for your reward in heaven is great [absolutely inexhaustible]; for in this same way they persecuted the prophets who were before you."

MATTHEW 5:6, 8, 10–12 AMP

14

GOD WANTS TO BLESS US

I n His Sermon on the Mount, Jesus presented to His disciples and all who were listening the code of behavior for His kingdom, a kingdom open to everyone who acknowledges Jesus as their Lord and Savior. And the wisdom of this sermon is timeless.

We will, for instance, be nourished by God's goodness when we hunger and thirst for His righteousness. We will know joy and God's blessing when we seek to be right with our precious Lord.

In addition, we will experience the blessing of being keenly aware of God's presence with us when we are "pure in heart," when we live with "integrity, moral courage, and godly character."

Believers will be blessed and "comforted by inner peace and God's love" when we face challenges in life, specifically those challenges that come because we are doing what is right and living as God calls us to live.

And we will be blessed to be "spiritually alive with life-joy in God's goodness" when people insult us and libel us because we are followers of Jesus.

Finally, we can be faithful when we remember that our ultimate reward awaits us in heaven no matter what we go through here on earth. Praise God for this ultimate promise of eternity with Him. Yes, we are blessed.

REFLECTION

This opening section of the Sermon on the Mount is called the Beatitudes. Which blessing in these beatitudes—or in the extended passage not quoted earlier—is most attractive to you? Why? What step(s) will you take to experience that blessing?

Jesus sent out these twelve, instructing them . . .
"Go to the lost sheep of the house of Israel. And as
you go, preach, saying, 'The kingdom of heaven is
at hand.' Heal the sick, raise the dead, cleanse the
lepers, cast out demons. Freely you have received,
freely give."

MATTHEW 10:5–8 AMP

15

OUR MISSION IN LIFE

Look again at what Jesus commanded His disciples when He sent them out to minister among the Jews. Jesus was not only talking to His first-century disciples but also giving us an example of how we are to live and serve Him.

Let me ask you a question. When was the last time you spoke to someone about salvation or, more specifically, about their relationship with Jesus Christ? Jesus calls all of us to be God's witnesses. Sharing your faith does take a certain boldness and a degree of courage. But the wonderful truth is, the more you share your faith, the more comfortable you'll be doing it next time.

When I was younger, I rarely talked with my friends about my love for Jesus. But as I got older and as my walk with the Lord became closer, the more I wanted to tell people what Jesus means to me. Today, I look for every opportunity to share the love of Jesus with everyone, using my words as well as my actions. Who doesn't need to know that Jesus loves us and will accept us just the way we are?

Yes, with all of our shortcomings and despite all of our mistakes in life, Jesus loves you, and He wants to be your Savior and Lord, your Shepherd and Friend.

REFLECTION

Before you became a follower of Jesus, who talked to you about salvation, Jesus, and His love? May reflecting on those people and the significance of those conversations motivate you to talk to others about Him.

Since we have been justified [that is, acquitted of sin, declared blameless before God] by faith, [let us grasp the fact that] we have peace with God [and the joy of reconciliation with Him] through our Lord Jesus Christ (the Messiah, the Anointed). Through Him we also have access by faith into this [remarkable state of] grace in which we [firmly and safely and securely] stand. Let us rejoice in our hope and the confident assurance of [experiencing and enjoying] the glory of [our great] God [the manifestation of His excellence and power].

ROMANS 5:1–2 AMP

16

PEACE WITH MY FATHER

STEVE STURGES

Those of us who have received forgiveness of sins and named Jesus Christ our Savior and Lord are, by faith, blessed with the peace of God. The war is over. Because of the sacrificial death and glorious resurrection of Christ, enmity between our sinful souls and holy God is removed. We are blessed by the miracle of this peace with God now and for eternity. In fact, we can call Him "Abba, Daddy" when we approach Him. In the following heartfelt story, Steve Sturges, a colleague in the In His Grip golf ministry, shares a story about his relationship with his earthly father that teaches an important lesson about our relationship with our heavenly Father.

I n the fall of 1983, I was a sophomore at the University of Oklahoma studying pre-med. Like many college students, I was busy searching for all the important things like the cheapest beer and the meaning of life. Translation: I really didn't know diddly about squat. Truth is, I needed God.

That same semester I was taking a class called Philosophy of Religion, taught by Dr. Tom Boyd. During one of his lectures, Dr. Boyd channeled his inner Methodist minister: "Have you ever argued with God?" To me, that was a silly question. Argue with an untouchable God? Really silly! Dr. Boyd quickly followed up: "Are you afraid that He can't take it? Trust me: He can." I was intrigued, but I didn't quite buy it.

At that time, my dad and I were like two trains on different tracks: we rarely communicated. He enjoyed drinking, smoking, and eating. A lot. Exercise meant taking a flight of stairs. He wore stress like a straitjacket. I was a nonsmoking, healthy-eating twenty-one-year-old exercise advocate who definitely wanted to avoid my dad's mistakes. Yes, I was the perfect combination of pride and rebellion. Our differences separated us more than the miles between home and school. Then December 9 happened. My father went to bed early, had a heart attack, and never woke up. He was fifty years old.

Mom, the rock of our family, called to deliver the

news about Dad. At first, I didn't recognize her voice. This was the first time someone close to me had died.

Just a few weeks earlier, Dad had flown in for OU Dad's Weekend. My brother John and I had thoroughly enjoyed spending time with him. After I got off the phone with my mom, I was haunted by a memory from that visit playing on an endless loop: as he boarded his flight back home, Dad had paused on the ramp and turned back to look at us one final time. He had tears in his eyes. Dad didn't cry. Ever.

That was the last time I would ever see him.

I quickly packed a suitcase and flew home to Arizona. Dr. Boyd's question tumbled in my head like a boot in a dryer. I was furious at God. Losing my dad when I had unfinished business with him must be God's fault. I was just beginning to appreciate him.

Arriving home, I spent some time trying to comfort Mom and then headed out for a walk. Under the stars— and prompted by Dr. Boyd's question—I raged at God: "How could You let this happen *now*?!" The Almighty and I argued for a mile or two. At least, *I* argued. God just listened. He wasn't offended by my accusation. Instead, He did what He's done throughout my life: He took my pain and carried it for me. He shared my sorrow. That night I realized what God truly wanted from me: a relationship. He didn't bring Dad back. God did something better: He showed up huge in a deeply personal way.

God wept with me just as He did at Lazarus's tomb. That night, I went to God looking for war . . . and found peace.

REFLECTION

When have you argued with or raged at God? What was His response? What impact did His response have on you? If you have never let God know that you were angry with Him, why not?

We have had earthly fathers who disciplined us, and we submitted and respected them [for training us]; shall we not much more willingly submit to the Father of spirits, and live [by learning from His discipline]? For our earthly fathers disciplined us for only a short time as seemed best to them; but He disciplines us for our good, so that we may share His holiness. For the time being no discipline brings joy, but seems sad and painful; yet to those who have been trained by it, afterwards it yields the peaceful fruit of righteousness [right standing with God and a lifestyle and attitude that seeks conformity to God's will and purpose].

HEBREWS 12:9–11 AMP

17

RECEIVING PEACE BEYOND UNDERSTANDING

BRUCE PULVER

During Wednesday night meetings with some twenty men involved in In His Grip, I had the pleasure of getting to know Bruce Pulver. Here he shares his experience with his mother and father and of the impact of their passing.

Ever find yourself in that lonely space between anger and sadness? It's not a pleasant place to be, is it? Yet in this no-man's land, God blessed me with peace beyond my understanding.

I had twenty-two positive, gratitude-filled years with Mom before she passed. On the day she gave birth to me, God took control and saved both our lives during the major heart trauma she experienced. She lived a full life with joy. Sadly, her heart stopped two months before my college graduation. Dorothy Marie Pulver had wanted to see her youngest son receive his diploma. This was not to be.

I later thought surely God would intervene in Dad's battle with dementia just as He did when He restored Mom's health. We just needed to pray, and God would heal Dad too, right? Sadly, this also was not to be.

Dad fought that battle for ten years. Then, six months before the birth of my first child, my dad's overwhelming wisdom, sharp wit, and iron-clad passion for helping others was gone. The disease took him. My heart cried out again. Now our first child would live in this world without the influence of either my dad, the greatest teacher I ever knew, or my mom, the great fighter who was a source of unstoppable optimism and gratitude.

I wrestled with God. I wanted to understand something that made no sense to me. *How could the parents who gave me tools and skills for life not be here to share and teach their grandchild? Why wouldn't God want that?*

After Dad's graveside service, the minister approached me. He had known Dad but had never met me. I had moved away after college to embark on my own life and career. Dad always said his job as a parent was to prepare his children to fly from the nest. So there was no way the pastor could understand the depth of my loss or my crippling pain of the emptiness I felt. My child would not feel the joy and love of my parents' teaching, never see their many ways of giving and caring, never hear their words of gratitude for life and their appreciation of God's many blessings.

The minister and I exchanged guarded pleasantries. But in my ears rang the unforgettable weeping of heart-broken family members and close friends. The images of the grave site, the nearby casket, and the imminent burial consumed me. *Why?*

My voice filled with sorrow, I offered the minister some thoughts for the memorial service he would conduct the next day. Speaking with wisdom gained during his years of pastoring, he said, "Bruce, you should step up tomorrow and speak about your father." *BAM!* When the initial shock subsided, I felt a tingle of peace begin to vibrate inside me. As I accepted the assignment to honor my father, I felt the Holy Spirit moving through me.

Without knowing at all how to write this eulogy, I opened the treasure chest of lessons my father had taught me. The words flowed freely, and I used pen and paper to capture them all. As I wrote, my focus changed from the mindset of a student to that of a teacher. I developed a sort of lesson plan for communicating what my parents taught me by how they lived. What once felt like an ending was turning into a fresh beginning.

The ten hours between talking to the minister and going to the memorial service where I would speak moved in slow motion. I was granted that time to think, write, put behind me my anger, and harness the powerful sadness for strength. After I finished the draft, I realized now was the time for me to become a teacher. I realized that my earthly father and my heavenly Father had prepared me to step up, call on God for guidance, and teach others what my parents and my God had taught me.

After the pain of great loss came a peace beyond my understanding.

REFLECTION

Often we experience God's peace that passes understanding when we're worried, fearful, or anxious. He also gives us His peace in times of loss and pain. When, if ever, have you experienced the gift of God's amazing peace when you were dealing with pain? Comment on the timing of that gift. Describe the impact it had on you.

"Come to Me, all you who labor and are heavy laden, and I will give you rest. Take My yoke upon you and learn from Me, for I am gentle and lowly in heart, and you will find rest for your souls. For My yoke is easy and My burden is light."

MATTHEW 11:28–30

18

MY ULTIMATE GOAL, HIS ULTIMATE GIFT

ANNE GRAHAM LOTZ

I have known Anne Graham Lotz for more than twenty years. I have watched her grow as an author and speaker, and I have had the privilege of publishing several of her gift books. She truly walks with God and is faithful to her calling to boldly write and talk about what Christ means to her.

M y life's goal is to know God better today than I did yesterday, better tomorrow than I do today. I want my life to bring God glory. I want to know Him and to make Him known, so that when people see me, they will want to know Jesus because of what they see of Him in my life. It's possible to achieve this goal if I am sick or well, rich or poor, loved or rejected, young or old. I can also achieve it as I submit to surgery for cancer; as I sit in a hospital waiting for chemotherapy; as I lie on a radiation bed. I can bring God glory speaking at my father's funeral or kneeling at my husband's grave or preaching from a podium or fixing a meal for my family.

In the Old Testament, Moses told God that he wanted to see His glory (Exodus 33:18). So God told Moses to stand in the cleft of a rock. Once Moses was in position, God put His hand over this faithful servant so he could feel the Lord's presence. Then God passed by, removed His hand, and told Moses he could see only the backside of His glory: "My face shall not be seen" (v. 23).

Like Moses, when you and I long to see God and reflect His glory, He may also put us in the cleft of a rock . . . in a hard place like a disease, divorce, death, or other disaster. We may initially feel His presence, but then He may remove His hand and allow us to feel abandoned . . . utterly alone. In that moment, we may not sense God's presence at all, but when we look back on that experience, we see the glory of God's character; we are able to recognize His faithfulness, mercy, truth, goodness, and love. In retrospect, we realize that God has been with us all along.

So be encouraged. One day we will be in heaven where there will be no more hard places of death, disease, or disasters; no more tears or grief or sickness or pain.

Old things are going to be wiped away, and everything will be made brand-new. Best of all, our desire to know God will be fulfilled. We will not see just the backside of God's glory; we will see His face (Revelation 21:3–4; 22:4)!

And that will be heaven . . . the ultimate gift of God's peace!

REFLECTION

Think about a time when you looked back on a hard place and realized that God had been with you all along. What may have kept you from that awareness in the moment? Why is this retrospective look significant to you?

Listen to counsel and receive instruction,
That you may be wise in your latter days.
There are many plans in a man's heart,
Nevertheless the Lord's counsel—that will
stand.

PROVERBS 19:20–21

19

LISTENING TO GOD

DR. JAMES LAW

I have had the privilege of knowing and working with Jim Law for thirteen years. Because of Jim's faithfulness and diligence, we at Thomas Nelson have been able to publish devotionals with fifty-two pastors each year. Jim is a man of God who listens to the Lord, especially when he faces major decisions and asks for divine guidance.

I will never forget when I had to make a life-altering decision that would significantly affect my family and me. It was a time of great stress and even some fear for all of us.

I had served at Westside Baptist Church in Jacksonville, Florida, for more than ten years. We absolutely loved that ministry and our congregation. The church was thriving and growing, and people's lives were being changed. God was moving in a remarkable way.

My wife and I both had family members in the church. Jacksonville was our hometown, and all our relatives were local. We had the perfect situation. We thought all our ministry years would be right there, and we were so happy and content to do just that.

But then Pastor Johnny Hunt at First Baptist Church Woodstock (Georgia) approached me about the possibility of joining him as the executive pastor. I immediately said, "I'm very happy where I'm serving. Thank you, but I'm not interested."

Pastor Hunt responded with a question: "Don't you think you should pray about it?"

I agreed to do so, but I did not think my decision would change.

After several months of praying, we began to sense the leadership of the Lord but were resisting the idea of leaving the church we loved. Someone suggested to me that I do what he does when he faces a big decision: Draw a line down the middle of a piece of paper and list the "pros" on one side and the "cons" on the other. Then carefully study it. Then throw away that piece of paper, get on your face before God, and say, "God, I desire Your perfect will and want to experience Your perfect peace, so I need You—and I ask You—to please tell me what to do."

My wife and I began to pray that short and simple prayer. After several weeks, God began to overwhelm us with His perfect peace as He made clear that His will for us was to minister in Woodstock, Georgia. We knew that, and we both arrived at that decision through prayer and Bible study. Even after we came to that decision, though, we struggled. Our decision was strictly an act of obedience. This choice was not our preference, but we knew what God had told us.

We obeyed our Lord. As a result, we have been overwhelmed by His peace that passes all understanding. I shudder to think about the many years of blessings we would have missed if we had not obeyed.

REFLECTION

When, if ever, has obedience to God meant doing exactly what you did *not* want to do? Think about the journey to the decision you made. Note the role God's peace played in this season.

Now the mind of the flesh is death [both now and forever—because it pursues sin]; but the mind of the Spirit is life and peace [the spiritual well-being that comes from walking with God—both now and forever]; the mind of the flesh [with its sinful pursuits] is actively hostile to God. It does not submit itself to God's law, since it cannot, and those who are in the flesh [living a life that caters to sinful appetites and impulses] cannot please God.

ROMANS 8:6–8 AMP

20

A LIFE THAT PLEASES GOD

Have you ever wondered how people who don't know God or follow Jesus drag themselves out of bed in the morning? Or maybe not that long ago you didn't know God and weren't following Jesus. Life without God is—according to Paul—a life ruled by the flesh, and our flesh "caters to sinful appetites and impulses" of our carnal nature. Living according to the demands of one's flesh can never please or satisfy God; never will He find it acceptable.

Think about that last sentence! There is nothing an unsaved person can do to please God. No good works, no religious observances, no sacrificial service, absolutely nothing. Yet God offers unsaved people (and that's all of us at some point) a way out of that empty, pointless, hopeless life. First, the unsaved must accept and acknowledge their status as guilty sinners and then, in a specific act of faith, receive Christ. Only then can the once-unsaved win God's smile of approval. When individuals are born again, though, they are no longer in the flesh, but in the Spirit. Let me explain.

Just as fish live in water and human beings live in air, believers live in the Spirit. However, the Spirit lives in each one of them also. Christ is actually in the believer. In fact, if someone is not indwelled by the Spirit of Christ, that person does not belong to Christ.

But when we name Jesus our Savior, His Spirit comes to dwell within us. As a result of that gift, we can rest in the complete assurance that our salvation is sealed for eternity. We can also live a life filled with the Lord's peace that passes all understanding. What a wonderful gift from our wonderful God!

REFLECTION

Just as fish live in water and human beings live in air, believers live in the Spirit, and the Spirit lives in each one of them. What impact does—or could— this truth have on your daily life? Be specific.

Let us pursue the things which make for peace and the things by which one may edify another. Do not destroy the work of God for the sake of food. All things indeed are pure, but it is . . . good neither to eat meat nor drink wine nor do anything by which your brother stumbles or is offended or is made weak.

ROMANS 14:19–21

21

STUMBLING

Have you ever considered that what you eat or drink can cause someone to stumble, question how well they can live out their faith, and be drawn away from the Lord?

The subjects in God's kingdom are not intended to be known primarily as foodies, gourmets, or wine connoisseurs. Instead, each of our lives should be characterized by practical righteousness, inner peace, relational harmony, and the presence of the Holy Spirit. It is a holy life that honors God. (As set forth earlier, what a man eats or doesn't eat is less important to God than the impact that action has on the people around the one eating.)

Again, a holy life honors God. Those followers who—in dependence on the Holy Spirit—try to live with righteousness, peace, and joy are honoring God by obeying His teachings and reflecting Jesus' example. So instead of bickering over inconsequential matters, we who have named Jesus our Savior and Lord should make every effort to maintain harmony in our Christian fellowship. Instead of causing others to stumble by insisting on our rights and freedoms, we should strive to build up our brothers and sisters in Christ and to help strengthen their most holy faith.

God is doing a work in each of His children. It is a thousand times better to refrain from meat or wine than to offend a brother or cause him to stumble spiritually. Giving up one's legitimate rights is a small price to pay for the spiritual well-being of a weaker or newer believer. It is better to exercise that liberty in private when no one could possibly be offended. That's simply the right thing to do.

REFLECTION

What are some twenty-first-century equivalents to the early church's issues of eating meat offered to idols and drinking wine? Which of your behaviors, if any, might cause fellow believers to stumble, to question how to live out their faith in a way that honors God? Ask God to help you change those.

Believers, whatever is true, whatever is honorable and worthy of respect, whatever is right and confirmed by God's word, whatever is pure and wholesome, whatever is lovely and brings peace, whatever is admirable and of good repute; if there is any excellence, if there is anything worthy of praise, think continually on these things [center your mind on them, and implant them in your heart]. The things which you have learned and received and heard and seen in me, practice these things [in daily life], and the God [who is the source] of peace and well-being will be with you.

PHILIPPIANS 4:8–9 AMP

22

WHAT'S ON YOUR MIND?

Our thoughts guide our decisions, shape our perceptions, and determine who we will become. If we let thoughts like those listed earlier rule our lives, we will know God's peace and the well-being He provides. For that to happen, we need to guard our thoughts and dwell on what is good.

When, for instance, we spend time with the Lord, we are in His presence and reminded of who He is. Having focused on His infinite power, goodness, and love, we just may find ourselves not worrying about the life issues that seemed so big before we entered into our heavenly Father's presence. Also, when we go to God in prayer, the Lord meets us with His mercy, His grace, and often a certain contentment that only He can give.

Clearly, we only gain when we let our minds dwell on things that are pure and lovely and "of good repute." Also, this right thinking helps lead to right living. When our thought lives are pure, odds are better that our lives will be pure. Finally, when we focus our thoughts on such things, "the God [who is the source] of peace and well-being will be with [us]." When would we not welcome that?

REFLECTION

Take an inventory of what you read, the podcasts and radio programs you listen to, and the television shows and movies you watch. Score each item on a scale of 1 (impure; vulgar) to 10 (pure). Then evaluate how you're doing. Also brainstorm some sources of thoughts that are honorable, right, biblical, lovely, calming, admirable, excellent, or praiseworthy. Choose one or two to add to your reading and listening plans this week.

"Do not worry about your life, what you will eat or what you will drink; nor about your body, what you will put on. Is not life more than food and the body more than clothing? Look at the birds of the air, for they neither sow nor reap nor gather into barns; yet your heavenly Father feeds them. Are you not of more value than they?"

MATTHEW 6:25-26

23

THE FAITHFUL PROVIDER

JIMMY HOUSTON

My friend Jimmy Houston is a fun-loving fisherman who loves the Lord and lives for Him each and every day. Jimmy has been a professional fisherman for over twenty-five years and has won countless fishing tournaments. Here, he talks about facing difficulties and trusting the Lord.

My wife, Chris, and I have been tested financially several times in our life. What I mean is, we've been completely broke!

Chris and I worked our way through college, each working sixty to eighty hours every week. We knew about sacrificing, working hard, and having very little. After college, we began working eighty to one hundred hours every week, and by the time we were in our early forties, God had blessed us with a successful business.

We had money in the bank, and basically everything we owned was paid for. What could go wrong? Well, plenty!

The Internal Revenue Service contacted us and explained they were changing the way we calculated our taxes. We had done nothing wrong, but a change needed to be made because of the size of our company—and this change would be retroactive for three years. Well, since day one of our television show, we had taken product in lieu of cash from some of the show's sponsors. We didn't pay taxes on that product until we sold it. Now, with the IRS-mandated change, we had to pay taxes on all the merchandise we had, in full, whether or not we had sold it. Our IRS bill—including penalties and interest—was over $400,000!

We were devastated. We didn't have that kind of money. I didn't want to wake up in the morning. I told Chris we were stopping the television show and fishing in national tournaments. I never wanted to pay another penny in taxes!

Then my God, whom I serve, stepped in.

Since my mid-twenties I've read the Bible through every year. Once our IRS bill arrived, it seemed that suddenly every day's reading was about my problem with them. In fact, I realized I could pick up a Bible, open it anywhere, and find God speaking to me about my financial problem.

Whenever I turned the radio dial, I'd somehow stop on a station with a preacher speaking directly to me about my problem. Was God working? Well, He had definitely gotten my attention and had me thinking . . .

My friend Jim Dawson, president of Brunswick Corporation, called and asked me to speak at a men's business luncheon. I declined and told him I was going through something so rough that I couldn't be positive to that group about God; I was too depressed. Being a great man of God as well as a great salesman, Jim talked me into it. That day, God used words I spoke to help others help me solve my problem, my disappointment, my depression. God was telling me it was all going to be okay.

That peace beyond all understanding settled in as I was speaking. I don't remember exactly what I said, but I was absolutely certain about the step I should take. Chris and I cashed in every CD, closed every bank account, and sold every stock. As a result, we had almost exactly $400,000—and we had *not* lost our house, our business, or any personal property. We had only lost all our money, but God gave me peace. In His time, He restored to me—as He did to Job—much more than we lost.

REFLECTION

When has serving others while you're going through hard times been a blessing to you? Give God glory by sharing a time when He provided for you in a surprising way.

Believers, rejoice! Be made complete [be what you should be], be comforted, be like-minded, live in peace [enjoy the spiritual well-being experienced by believers who walk closely with God]; and the God of love and peace [the source of lovingkindness] will be with you.

2 CORINTHIANS 13:11 AMP

24

A BLESSED PROMISE

I n Paul's second letter to the Corinthians, he offered believers instructions for how to live in peace with one another. He emphasized that we should live in agreement with each other, encouraging one another, and being of one mind. If we do this, we will live in peace and "the God of love . . . will be with [us]."

Clearly, how we treat one another matters. We can only reflect to the world the goodness and love of our God when we are kind and considerate to our Christian brothers and sisters. When we choose to obey the charges of 2 Corinthians 13:11—when we choose unity and sacrificial love for others—God will bless us with His peace that passes our understanding. Our heavenly Father will also guide and enable us to live in a way that brings honor and glory to Him.

Obedience to the call to be "what you should be," receive God's comfort, be like-minded, and enjoy the spiritual well-being that comes with walking closely with God ensures quality of life for believers and for the nonbelievers around them. Furthermore, the choice to live God's way also means the blessing of this promise fulfilled: "the God of love and peace . . . will be with you." Amen and amen.

REFLECTION

Paul called believers to be "what you should be," receive God's comfort, be like-minded, and enjoy the spiritual well-being that comes with walking closely with God. Which of those four areas do you want to work on this week? What steps will you take toward that goal?

Blessed be the God and Father of our Lord Jesus Christ, the Father of mercies and God of all comfort, who comforts us in all our tribulation, that we may be able to comfort those who are in any trouble, with the comfort with which we ourselves are comforted by God.

2 CORINTHIANS 1:3-4

25

PEACE WHEN TRAGEDY STRIKES

BRIAN JORGENSON

Through the ministry of In His Grip, I've had the privilege of getting to know Brian Jorgenson. All of us who know Brian were shocked to hear of his wife's tragic death. Despite that painful loss, Brian's life testifies to God's grace and provision. God is always there to comfort us, to strengthen us, and to carry us when we can't take a step on our own.

My definition of *peace* is knowing that God has you covered because you gave your life over to Him when you accepted Jesus as your Savior.

My most significant peace moment came on Sunday, August 26, 2018, when seven state troopers showed up at my front door. It was 7:30 p.m., and they had come to tell me my amazing wife and my two kids' rock-star mom was just killed in a car accident while on her way to Memphis, Tennessee, for work.

When a truck going the opposite direction had a tire blow out, it came across the median and hit my wife's car head-on. The officers said she was killed on impact and did not suffer. After they had shared the news with only me, I then gathered Connor and Riley so we could process the news together. For some reason the officers had the three of us sit on the side of my bed. There, they broke the news to the children as I held them tightly to my sides.

Neither the officers nor my children knew that this was the very spot where only seven months prior—on January 14, 2018—I was on my knees in prayer, crying out to the Lord for help. Right then and there I had decided to give everything up to the Lord because, simply put, my life was out of control. My awakening started when my daughter, Riley, wrote me a letter and laid it on my pillow while I was in the shower that night. In this letter my fifteen-year-old daughter was direct as she explained exactly what she thought of me as her dad and as a husband to her mom. As I was reading that letter, the guilt and shame I felt took me to my knees. After I stood up and realized my next steps, it was as if a million-pound weight had been lifted from my body. I was reborn with the Holy Spirit as my Guide and Jesus as my Savior. And that peace I experienced on August 26 was the peace I experienced on January 14 when I gave every aspect of my life to my Lord and Savior Jesus Christ.

For some reason my children held me so tight as the officers spoke. Even as we sat listening to their every word, I had a peace about me that everything was going to be okay. I knew that the Holy Spirit would surround us and guide us as we handled this tragedy. I didn't falter in my belief that God is good and that He had His hand on us that day—and that He would do so every day.

As I write this, it will soon be three years since Jesus called our beautiful Patricia home, but not one day goes by when I am not thankful for my Lord and Savior. Without His being such a big part of my life, I don't know how I would have navigated the biggest loss of my life.

REFLECTION

Looking back over your life, what season can you not imagine navigating without the Lord? Comment on the role He played in your life at that time—and thank Him. Also note what you learned about His comfort that enables you to more effectively comfort others.

Now the LORD had said to Abram:

"Get out of your country,
From your family
And from your father's house,
To a land that I will show you." . . .

So Abram departed as the LORD had spoken to
him.

GENESIS 12:1, 4

26

GO!

DR. DON WILTON

I have had the privilege of knowing Pastor Don Wilton for the past twenty years. This South African native is a true man of God, and I love his accent and eloquence in the way he communicates. For the past fifteen years of Pastor Billy Graham's life, Dr. Wilton had the honor of serving as his pastor. He spent every Saturday with Billy as they shared life together.

After Billy's death, I asked Dr. Wilton if he would write a book and share his experiences on those Saturdays. He agreed, and his book, *Saturdays with Billy*, is now in print. Dr. Wilton shares his ministry story in his own eloquent style.

T he futile search raged on in the deep of my heart. What I wanted seemed completely elusive.
Give me peace, I cried out . . . without crying out.

There she stood. My bride was so beautiful and so perfect in every way. Even her hair smiled at me as I gazed upon her with gratitude to my God—and not without an inner sense of self-congratulations. *How could I not have peace?*

The apartment was perfect as well. The right bed and the right table and the right seat all fit snuggly in exactly the right place. She was so gifted.

The car shone like a star from heaven, and the motorbike sat waiting to be mounted. Soon we two lovebirds roared off high up into the mountains of the eastern cape of southern Africa. We'd filled our backpack with an assortment of chocolates, scones, and snacks designed to complement the magnificent views that barked like hyenas when the sun came up and yawned like a sleepy hippopotamus when the sun went down. I noted that even the natural world around us was at peace.

University degrees began to accumulate, we accepted scholarships to study overseas, and we enjoyed the constant sounds of the Indian Ocean.

Yet the restlessness I felt was ever-present. I chose the immersion of self in life as the logical antidote for this inexplicable condition. I threw myself into sports, coaching, teaching, and running. I went to church most of the time. Other times, I didn't. I certainly did not make it a priority. I was good with Jesus for sure. My salvation was secure; I was not at all in doubt. Totally secure in Christ but not at peace in Christ.

The accolades built up, but the longing remained. Ways to satisfy that longing came and went. Serving in church could be the key, I thought, so I served as a deacon. I preached the Word most Sundays to a wonderful (small) congregation of really terrific and appreciative people. But still I had no peace.

Then it happened. One day, a preacher from America visited our church service. My wife and I did some business with the one true God and Father of our Lord and Savior Jesus Christ.

"I am calling you," He said.

"Me?" I asked.

"Yes, you."

"To do what?" I asked.

"To get up, sell all you have, and go to a land I will show you."

I said, "Yes, Lord."

And she said, "Yes, Lord."

"But how can this be?" we said to each other—and to Him. "We have very little money. We don't know where to go or who will meet us if we do go wherever it is You want us to go."

A strange thing happened. I noticed an inner peace that had eluded me all my life. Yet these circumstances made no sense whatsoever. They certainly weren't the source of peace!

We resigned our positions and gave up our salaries. Then my wife said, "If we sell everything, we may have enough to buy two plane tickets to New York City." Crazy wife! But again I noticed the peace.

Two months later, we purchased two tickets and arrived in New York City, USA, with two suitcases and barely $1,500 in our pockets.

The adventure had begun—and I knew peace as I never had before.

REFLECTION

When were you most surprised to notice that you were feeling a sense of peace? What did that experience teach you?

To those who have received and possess [by God's will] a precious faith of the same kind as ours, by the righteousness of our God and Savior, Jesus Christ: Grace and peace [that special sense of spiritual well-being] be multiplied to you in the [true, intimate] knowledge of God and of Jesus our Lord. For His divine power has bestowed on us [absolutely] everything necessary for [a dynamic spiritual] life and godliness, through true and personal knowledge of Him who called us by His own glory and excellence.

2 PETER 1:1-3 AMP

27

KNOWLEDGE, PEACE, POWER, AND TRANSFORMATION

Peter began his second letter with a lofty, prayerlike blessing for those who would hear these words: "[May] grace and peace . . . be multiplied to you in the . . . knowledge of God and of Jesus our Lord." This knowledge of God—this knowing Him, not just knowing *about* Him—gives us power to, day by day, live a godly life that honors Him.

Peter also wanted God's people to know the peace only He can give, peace defined here as "that special sense of spiritual well-being." And Peter didn't want God's people to have this knowledge of God or His peace in small doses! At the start of this letter, Peter made clear that He wanted these blessings "multiplied" and abundant.

Such multiplication of divine grace and peace happens as God blesses our knowledge of Him. In order to keep growing in our knowledge of our infinite and infinitely wonderful God, we would be wise to dwell in the secret place of the Most High rather than make only occasional visits there. Those who live in the sanctuary of faith rather than in its suburbs experience more fully God's grace and peace.

Next, in verse 3, Peter revealed how we Christians can lead a vibrant and victorious spiritual life in this dark and lost world. We can only do so because, according to Peter, God has, by His power and grace, "bestowed on us [absolutely] everything necessary for [a dynamic spiritual] life and godliness."

Just as God's power saves us in the first place, so His power energizes us to live holy lives from that point of salvation on. By His gospel plan and power, God saves us from the penalties of sin, which are eternal damnation, eternal death, and eternal separation from God. By knowing Him, continuing to know Him better, and walking in the power of His Spirit, we can find Him making us more like Jesus. In other words, the better we know Jesus, the more we become like Him.

REFLECTION

It's easier to see another person's progress in becoming more and more like Jesus. (The fancy word for that process is *sanctification.*) It's harder to see our own. Why do you think that's the case? Who can you ask who might give you a sense of how you are growing in your knowledge of God and/or how you are becoming more like Jesus? Grab coffee with that person.

God is not one to show partiality [to people as though Gentiles were excluded from God's blessing], but in every nation the person who fears God and does what is right [by seeking Him] is acceptable and welcomed by Him. . . . Through His name everyone who believes in Him [whoever trusts in and relies on Him, accepting Him as Savior and Messiah] receives forgiveness of sins.

ACTS 10:34–35, 43 AMP

28

PEACE WITH GOD FOR JEWS AND GENTILES ALIKE

Empowered by the Holy Spirit, Peter began this sermon to the Roman centurion Cornelius and all his family by clearly stating that God first shared the gospel message of forgiveness of sins, peace with God, and the promise of eternal life with the Jews. Saying that "God is not one to show partiality," Peter welcomed the Gentiles to hear the gospel as good news for them as well.

Peter's audience in Caesarea must have heard about Jesus of Nazareth—about His life of serving, healing, and teaching; about His crucifixion; and perhaps even some rumors about His resurrection. Then came the best news of all for his first audience: Peter taught that whoever believes in the name of the Messiah will receive remission of sins. God extends His gracious offer of forgiveness, relationship with Him, and eternal life not only to Israel but to Gentiles and all the world.

If you would like to know the forgiveness of your sins, simply confess them. Then believe that God hears and forgives (1 John 1:9), thank Him for His forgiveness made possible by Jesus' death on the cross (John 3:16), and, in faith, ask Jesus to be the Lord of your life. Find a Bible and a Bible-preaching church so you can worship, love and be loved, and grow in your relationship with Jesus.

REFLECTION

In Matthew 18:3–4, Jesus called His followers to "become as little children" if they are to "enter the kingdom of heaven." Why does Jesus call for childlike faith? What can we do to cultivate childlike faith in the good news of the gospel?

Blessed and worthy of praise be the God and Father of our Lord Jesus Christ, who has blessed us with every spiritual blessing in the heavenly realms in Christ, just as [in His love] He chose us in Christ [actually selected us for Himself as His own] before the foundation of the world, so that we would be holy [that is, consecrated, set apart for Him, purpose-driven] and blameless in His sight. In love He predestined and lovingly planned for us to be adopted to Himself as [His own] children through Jesus Christ, in accordance with the kind intention and good pleasure of His will—to the praise of His glorious grace and favor, which He so freely bestowed on us in the Beloved [His Son, Jesus Christ].

EPHESIANS 1:3–6 AMP

29

GOD'S FAVOR, OUR FREEDOM

In the earlier passage from Ephesians, Paul used some words and phrases—such as "chose us," "selected us," "predestined," and "planned for us"—that make a discussion of predestination and election inevitable. So here we go.

First of all, the doctrine of election—of God choosing who is saved—lets our sovereign God be sovereign, meaning He can do as He pleases, but He will never do anything unjust.

Second, if God left the human race alone, every single person would be lost. But does God have the right to show mercy only to some?

Adding to the complexity of this divine mystery, the Bible that teaches sovereign election means human responsibility. God extends salvation to all people everywhere (John 3:16; Romans 10:9). Anyone can be saved by repenting of sins and believing in the sinless life, sacrificial death, and victorious resurrection of the Lord Jesus Christ. So if a person is lost, it is because that person chooses to be lost, not because God desires it.

The fact is, the same Bible teaches both election *and* salvation to all who will receive it. Both doctrines are found in a single verse: "All that My Father gives Me will come to Me; and the one who comes to Me I will most certainly not cast out" (John 6:37 AMP). The first half of the verse speaks of God's sovereign choice; the last half extends the offer of mercy to everyone. The best policy for us is to believe both doctrines simply because the Bible teaches both. The truth is not found somewhere between election and mere free will; the truth is found in both extremes at the same time. The good pleasure of God's will is the sovereign nonfiction behind our predestination.

Even if we can't fully understand, much less explain, the mystery, we can camp on the answer to "Why did God save anyone?" Simply because it was His good pleasure to surround Himself with forgiven sinners, conformed to the image of His Son, who could spend eternity with Him.

REFLECTION

Why is it good that we can't fully understand
God or explain why He does what He does?

To the saints and faithful believers in Christ [who are] at Colossae: Grace to you and peace [inner calm and spiritual well-being] from God our Father.

We give thanks to God, the Father of our Lord Jesus Christ, as we pray always for you, for we have heard of your faith in Christ Jesus [how you lean on Him with absolute confidence in His power, wisdom, and goodness], and of the [unselfish] love which you have for all the saints (God's people).

COLOSSIANS 1:2–4 AMP

30

THE GOSPEL TRUTH

Paul addressed this letter to the Colossians specifically to "the saints and the faithful brethren in Christ" (NKJV). In that phrase are two New Testament terms that refer to all Christians. First, all believers are "saints," meaning that they are separated to God from the world and that, as a result, they should lead holy lives. "Faithful brethren" establishes that all believers are adopted children of a common Father because they have put their faith in the Lord Jesus.

Paul greeted these saints—these believing brothers and sisters—with a lovely salutation: "Grace to you . . . from God our Father." I can imagine the apostle falling to his knees in thanks and prayer, grateful for the faithful Colossians, the power of the gospel, and the unspeakable privilege of having an audience with the Sovereign of the universe. Paul also spoke openly that saving faith is faith in Christ Jesus. The Lord Jesus Christ is always set forth in Scripture as the object of faith. Faith in itself is not sufficient. Saving faith that enables us to have peace with God is faith that the sinless Lord Jesus Christ was crucified as the sacrificial Lamb, as payment for our sins, and then rose from the dead victorious over sin and death. When we embrace this gospel message, we enter into a personal life-giving relationship with this powerful, faithful, good God, and this relationship will last for all eternity.

REFLECTION

Spend some time reflecting on what it means that you are a saint . . . and that you are a brother/sister of Jesus. Consider what difference these truths could, maybe should, make on how you live. What evidence might people see that you are a saint? That you are a brother/sister of Jesus? What steps will you take and what changes will you make to live more like a saint and a sibling of your Lord?

I pray that you may have the power to comprehend, with all the saints, what is the breadth and length and height and depth, and to know the love of Christ that surpasses knowledge, so that you may be filled with all the fullness of God.

Now to him who by the power at work within us is able to accomplish abundantly far more than all we can ask or imagine, to him be glory in the church and in Christ Jesus to all generations, forever and ever. Amen.

EPHESIANS 3:18–21 NRSV

31

GREATER THAN WE ASK OR IMAGINE

BETH RYAN

I have had the privilege of working with Beth Ryan for the past twenty years. She is a creative genius, and the Spirit of God dwells in her heart and in her mind. May you find peace in her experience of having God supply our needs for His purpose.

Being a single mom when my children were young, I always tried to protect them and keep them involved in church.

In this one season of my life, we moved into a duplex, and I soon realized that the area was not the best environment, especially for little ones. One night I found myself wailing before God. I remember specifically crying out, "God, I know You love my children even more than I do. Please help me get out of this place!" Although

I cried myself to sleep that night, I was absolutely confident that God hears our prayers and answers them.

The next morning my sister called me. She told me that she had shared with a worker at a local church about my desperation to get away from where my kids and I were living. As a result of her sharing, I was about to see God "do exceedingly abundantly above all that we ask or think" (NKJV).

Unbeknownst to my sister, the person she had shared my story to owned a rental property. God moved his heart and—lo and behold!—he graciously offered me the house for the same amount I was paying in the less-desirable area. In fact, this man's rental was in an older neighborhood where I had always wanted to live; its old trees and longtime residents gave the place a sense of stability and peace.

Furthermore, across the street from this rental was a gentle grandfather figure who watched out for me and my kids for three years. Not only did Grandpa Rex keep watch over us, but he also had the best summer garden and was always giving me fresh vegetables. In addition, he sold me a car for little to nothing when my car broke down. I learned from that wonderful experience to fully walk in the truth of Philippians 4:6–7: "Don't worry about anything; instead, pray about everything. Tell

God what you need, and thank him for all he has done. Then you will experience God's peace, which exceeds anything we can understand. His peace will guard your hearts and minds as you live in Christ Jesus" (NLT).

It was not always easy being a single parent, but the Lord always provided. Even when I could not see or imagine what He was doing, He blessed me with the gift of peace, and that gift has kept me anchored to Him through the years and therefore free of worry and anxiety.

When we trust in the Lord and lean on Him, He will always answer our prayers and supply us with what He wants us to have. God is always faithful.

REFLECTION

Describe a time—or two or three—when God answered one of your prayers in a way far greater than you would have asked or imagined. Spend some time praising God for His goodness, His faithfulness, His grace, and His love.

Be anxious for nothing, but in everything by prayer and supplication, with thanksgiving, let your requests be made known to God; and the peace of God, which surpasses all understanding, will guard your hearts and minds through Christ Jesus.

PHILIPPIANS 4:6–7

32

IN EVERYTHING, PRAY

DR. JOHNNY HUNT

I have known Johnny Hunt for fourteen years, and he has served as the general editor of thirteen J. Countryman devotionals. In the time I've known him, I've seen his deep devotion to his ministry. Johnny works tirelessly to mentor young pastors who are preaching in churches everywhere. A bright light for our Lord, Johnny offers his mentees a true example of how a Christ-follower should live.

I remember a time in my life when I was wondering if there was anything the Lord wanted me to do. So I started asking the Lord to speak to me and make His plan clear to me. It wasn't long before I came upon Mark 9:29, a scripture that really challenged me. In that verse Jesus said, "This kind [of unclean spirit] can come out by nothing but prayer and fasting." As I meditated on this statement, I sensed the Lord calling me to Himself through prayer and fasting, so I made a commitment to do just that. It made sense to me that God would use this discipline to slow me down, help me focus on Him, and enable me to discern His purpose for my life. In this season I also journaled anything and everything I thought the Lord was saying to me. In Jeremiah 33:3, for instance, I noted this wonderful promise: "Call to Me, and I will answer you, and show you great and mighty things, which you do not know."

As I fasted and prayed, the Lord said things to me that I had never heard and revealed to me things about myself that I had never noticed. This time of fasting, studying Scripture, and journaling was also a time of confessing, repenting, and drawing near to God. One day I sensed He was telling me to do something: in my heart I sensed God calling me to mentor young pastors for the rest of my pastorate.

As I continued to pray, I found that I really desired two things in particular. First, I asked the Lord to allow peace to rule in my heart. Second, I asked Him to tell me who to work with and how to get this ministry running and then to make it last. I began brainstorming what this ministry would look like and exactly how I could do what I sensed God was calling me to do.

A visionary leader most of my ministry, I found it

natural to ask God for a clear vision of what this ministry might look like. Here is what I think I heard from the Lord:

- Mentor college graduates who are studying to become pastors.
- Look for a candidate's passion to feel; his sense of being called to work with me; and a whatever-it-takes mentality.
- Give each of them a travel allowance and a book allowance.

I still had questions:

- Where would these young men live?
- Would I pay them? If so, how much?
- How long would my basic mentoring program last?
- What would be the most effective teaching techniques?
- How many mentees could I train at a time?

As I prayed and fasted, the Lord gave me clear direction and sweet inner peace. He also answered each one of the questions above. As a result of the Lord's guidance about the program and the design He provided me, I have been privileged to mentor younger pastors for twenty-five years.

During this season of getting newly established in the battle, I realized an important truth. I saw played out in my life that whenever I obeyed His single first step for me, His answers to the rest of my questions became clear. The major lesson I learned along the way is that you don't have to have all the answers. Just obey what you do know to do, and—by God's grace—the rest will become clear.

REFLECTION

What is the purpose of fasting? Describe your experience with fasting and praying. What current situation, if any, might you better understand after a time of fasting and praying about it? Will you enter into a time of fasting and praying? Why or why not?

The Lord stood with me and strengthened me, so that the message might be preached fully through me, and that all the Gentiles might hear. Also I was delivered out of the mouth of the lion. And the Lord will deliver me from every evil work and preserve me for His heavenly kingdom. To Him be glory forever and ever. Amen!

2 TIMOTHY 4:17–18

33

THE LORD IS FAITHFUL

CHUCK WALLINGTON

I have known Chuck Wallington for over twenty years. He was a leader in management of his Christian bookstore, and he was always open to good marketing ideas. But most of all, he is a faithful man of God who has lived a good Christian life. His story is one of unwelcome hardships, sadness, and triumph. As you read Chuck's story, you will find an example of what it means to depend on the Lord, and you will see that He faithfully reassures us when we need it most.

I n August 2008, both my personal life and my business life were suddenly turned upside down when our banker called to tell us that our family-owned business had been the target of an almost $1 million embezzlement. We literally and instantaneously went from being one of the largest and most profitable stores in the

Christian retail industry to being deeply in debt, and we had no reserves.

Our faithful God sent many kind and generous friends who helped save our company from immediate collapse, yet—three years later—as we prepared to enter 2012, I still found myself stressing over whether or not our company and family would survive.

As I was leaving our store late one afternoon, I noticed a man in our book department and asked him if he needed assistance. He said, "No, but I do need to speak with you for just a moment."

Unsure what he might want and therefore more than a little uneasy, I looked into his face, and all my concerns and apprehension disappeared. His face was the most peaceful and comforting I had ever encountered. The man continued: "I didn't know who I was supposed to talk with when I came in today, but when I heard your voice, the Lord told me to speak to you."

Now, I need to explain that I was raised in a very traditional Southern Baptist church—but at times have been accused of being "Bapti-costal." Regardless of your theological background, such a statement will get your attention. He explained, "God sent me today to tell you that He says everything is going to be okay." Immediately, a peace washed over me, God's peace that I had not experienced since the financial crisis had hit our family business several years earlier.

When I left the store that afternoon, I felt as though a weight had been lifted. Through this unknown brother in Christ, God had spoken His peace into my turmoil and fear.

A few days later, one of our cashiers came to me after our staff's morning devotions and said she had something to give me. She had attended a Bible conference over the weekend and had purchased a book from one of the speakers for me. She shared that as she went through the line to get it signed, the author asked how to personalize it.

She said, "Please sign it 'To Chuck.' He's my boss."

The author immediately looked up and asked, "Is he involved in Christian publishing?"

Thinking the author might know me, our cashier responded that indeed I was and that I managed a Christian bookstore. After she gave him my full name, he explained that while he didn't know me and had never heard of me or our store, he had a word from the Lord for me. With that, he stood up, leaving others waiting in line for his signature, and asked her to follow him behind a curtain.

She quickly grabbed a piece of paper to record his

message for me word for word. I still have that piece of paper in my Bible, and from time to time—when I most need to be reminded—it falls out as I open my Bible. His statement is several lines long, but it begins and ends with "God says that everything is going to be okay," the *exact same words* that my visiting customer had spoken to me just days earlier.

I cherish to this day the fact that, just days apart, God used two different messengers to deliver those reassuring, peace-giving words. If you knew me, you'd understand why I believe God told some of His angels in heaven after that first messenger, "Chuck is rather dense. I probably need to send the message again, this time in writing."

You may hear in your spirit God speak through the still, calm voice of the Holy Spirit. Maybe you hear Him in the spoken words of a stranger or the written words of a fellow believer. However God reminds you of His peace, you undoubtedly know as I do that there is no substitute for His peace when there is any turmoil in your soul.

One more thing: Jesus' first words to His disciples on the evening of His resurrection, as they huddled in that locked upper room, so fearful and confused, were "Peace be to you" (John 20:26 NASB). Jesus still speaks

His peace into our lives, and I'm convinced you will hear Him if you listen.

REFLECTION

Describe the most dramatic time you sensed God speak His peace into your life. What was the most surprising time He blessed you with His peace? When, if ever, has He used you to speak peace to someone else? He may want you to slow down now and hear His words of peace to you, or He may want to let you know who needs to hear you speak words of peace to them.

Jesus and His disciples got into a boat, and He said to them, "Let us cross over to the other side of the lake (Sea of Galilee)." So they set out. But as they were sailing, He fell asleep. And a fierce gale of wind swept down [as if through a wind tunnel] on the lake, and they began to be swamped, and were in great danger. They came to Jesus and woke Him, saying, "Master, Master, we are about to die!" He got up and rebuked the wind and the raging, violent waves, and they ceased, and it became calm [a perfect peacefulness]. And He said to them, "Where is your faith [your confidence in Me]?" They were afraid and astonished, saying to one another, "Who then is this, that He commands even the winds and the sea, and they obey Him?"

LUKE 8:22–25 AMP

34

THROUGH THE STORMS OF LIFE

REGINA PRUDE

Regina Prude is the host of an XM Radio program called *The Leadership Zone.* She has invited me a few times to speak on the program. In addition to her beautiful radio presence, Regina always skillfully guides our conversation whenever I appear on her show.

What happens when storms change the entire trajectory of life? Storms can both erupt and interrupt. For many people, that's happening now. Incredibly, God speaks triumphantly both to us who are *in* the storm and *to* the storm itself.

When I faced the most challenging health crisis of my life, my heavenly Father spoke to me in the tumult. Like walking-on-water Peter who suddenly started to sink, I had run to Jesus in a panic. He stilled my storm . . . hushed the threatening waves . . . and astonished me with His power.

That storm was my 2001 diagnosis of stage 4 non-Hodgkin lymphoma. My husband and I decided to tell our congregation immediately. After all, we were a team, and we had been with this precious church for twenty-eight years. Our dear members needed to know what Pastor Floyd and his wife were going through.

As news spread, caring believers spoke words of deep concern—even if their faces sometimes reflected hidden doubts and fears. Too many seemed to be thinking, *You've definitely found yourself in a situation that's even too hard for God!*

And I felt that way, too, sometimes. Life can batter us, scar us. I felt pounded by my physical battle against cancer, by strength-draining emotional upheavals, and by stomach-churning fear when I considered the reality of what a stage 4 cancer diagnosis means.

Yet from the storms I faced early on, I learned a strategy that led me straight to God's peace. It's simply this: Stop. Praise! Pause. Be still; know that He is God.

I also spoke over my life and my health these three powerful affirmations about God. I still speak these affirmations over the lives of people I love as well as over whatever crisis next arrives at my doorstep.

1. God, You alone set my mind at ease. Your transforming power brings divine comfort. Holy Spirit, I listen for Your voice.
2. Your armor, Lord, wraps all around me. Your hand of protection holds me and those I love. No harm can come my way without Your permission.
3. Lord, because of Your resurrection, no opposing force can defeat me. No shadow can overcome me.

Speaking these encouragements helped me face down any doubt and deal with any event that threatened.

At the cancer clinic, I sat for hours as a chemotherapy cocktail, jazzed up with a medication just out of clinical trials, entered my body through an IV and coursed through my veins to do battle on my behalf. Throughout those chemo sessions, God's angels provided all the promised peace I needed.

I also claimed the unshakable joy of Jude's benediction: "Now to him who is able to keep you from falling, and to make you stand without blemish in the presence of his glory with rejoicing, to the only God our Savior, through Jesus Christ our Lord, be glory, majesty, power, and authority, before all time and now and forever. Amen" (Jude vv. 24–25 NRSV). Not one of God's promises is ever too much to claim.

And the warmth of the Lord's love always surrounds us when we receive His miracle of peace.

REFLECTION

In a single sentence, describe the greatest storm you've encountered in your life. Which of Regina's steps did you happen to take? Which of her steps would have been helpful? What will you take away from Regina's account for the next storm that comes your way?

God forbid that I should boast except in the cross of our Lord Jesus Christ, by whom the world has been crucified to me, and I to the world. For in Christ Jesus neither circumcision nor uncircumcision avails anything, but a new creation.

And as many as walk according to this rule, peace and mercy be upon them, and upon the Israel of God.

GALATIANS 6:14–16

35

PEACE FROM ABOVE

ROLAND COLSON

Roland Colson is my brother in Christ. I got to know him at church when I was urging every member of the Sunday school class I taught to serve in the church. Roland did just that and offered his time and talent to serve. Roland also served by writing and posting on Facebook a daily devotional called "God's Word Last Word."

Peace of mind is important to most people. Many of us will do almost anything to experience it. Some people will travel to exotic places at great financial expense. Others will inject brain-altering drugs into their bodies or pursue New Age interests like astrology, psychic readings, and the presence of spiritual energy in physical objects like mountains or trees. But such practices are not the true path to peace.

A few years ago, I was on top of the world. I was the

warden of a maximum-security prison that housed every death-row inmate in the state. It also housed the state's most hardened and dangerous criminals.

In addition to managing the prison, I felt as though I was in total control of everything going on in my life. Family was good. I was blessed with good friends and neighbors. Then one night, at 2:00 a.m., my wife got up to use the restroom. She stepped into the hallway and collapsed. Falling, she hit the floor hard and stopped breathing.

I called 911, got down on my knees, and began to pray—and my wife began to breathe. An ambulance arrived within minutes. The attendants placed her on a stretcher, told me there wasn't any room in the ambulance for me, and took off for the hospital. I followed behind in my own car.

We barely made it outside the prison grounds when the ambulance pulled over, stopped, and turned off the lights and the siren. I thought to myself, *She's gone . . . she has died.* I once again turned to God in prayer. The lights came back on, the siren wailed, and we sped off again toward the hospital.

Doctors rushed my wife through the emergency room, and she wound up in intensive care. An ulcer had ruptured, and my wife had already lost over five pints of blood. She shouldn't have survived.

Most of life is outside our control. We sit in gridlock traffic for hours upon hours and miss an important event. A mother sits in her child's hospital room praying for a miracle that may never occur. When things like this—big or small—happen, we can become frustrated and completely lose our peace.

But Christ granted me peace that day my wife fell. It wasn't something I could barter with God and receive. It wasn't something I could earn, and I didn't have to beg for it. God's peace was a simple gift He offered me, a gift I could have denied. But on that fateful day, I said yes, and God blessed me with a peace that only He could give.

"I'm telling you these things while I'm still living with you. The Friend, the Holy Spirit whom the Father will send at my request, will make everything plain to you. He will remind you of all the things I have told you. I'm leaving you well and whole. That's my parting gift to you. Peace. I don't leave you the way you're used to being left—feeling abandoned, bereft. So don't be upset. Don't be distraught." (John 14:25–27 MSG)

REFLECTION

When, if ever, have you encountered death, yet experienced peace? Describe that time and then note why peace is a great gift at the time of a person's death.

"You will keep in perfect and constant peace the one whose mind is steadfast [that is, committed and focused on You—in both inclination and character],
Because he trusts and takes refuge in You [with hope and confident expectation].
"Trust [confidently] in the LORD forever [He is your fortress, your shield, your banner],
For the LORD GOD is an everlasting Rock [the Rock of Ages]."

ISAIAH 26:3–4 AMP

36

MY LORD, MY ROCK

Among the many blessings God gives His people is His perfect peace. When we walk with God and seek to follow in the footsteps of Jesus, being obedient and choosing to yield to God's will, He will bless us with—among other things—His perfect peace.

We walk more closely with God when we have committed ourselves to the Lord and made Him the center of our lives. In other words, we must surrender our lives to God, let Him guide our decisions, and honor Him in all we say and do.

In addition, the Lord designed us to be in relationship with Him and to enjoy a heart-to-heart closeness with Him. Yet God will never force Himself on us. Instead, He waits for our response. When we do, however, come to know God intimately and love Him deeply, we experience contentment and joy and, yes, peace. To live the Christian life is to allow Jesus to live His life in us and through us. That means that all we accomplish we do through His Spirit, and that kind of wonderful partnership results in peace. God has promised to keep us in perfect peace when we place our trust in Him. Christ is our peace. His presence with us is the presence of His peace within us.

So, a quick review. What is the peace that this passage speaks of, that this book focuses on? I think of the peace that God gives as the inner sense of contentment and quietness we have regardless of life's circumstances. This peace is rooted in our confidence in our ever-faithful heavenly Father. It is the presence of joy in the midst of whatever we encounter in life. A person walking closely with God and resting in the peace He gives can endure an avalanche of hardship and difficulty. After all, the Spirit of our holy, omnipotent, all-wise, and never-changing God lives within us.

REFLECTION

Name two or three experiences that built your confidence in your heavenly Father's faithfulness and love. Into what current situation do you need to be confident in Him? What will that look like?

"*I am the* LORD, *and there is no other;*
There is no God besides Me.
I will gird you, though you have not known Me,
That they may know from the rising of the sun
       to its setting
That there is none besides Me.
I am the LORD, *and there is no other;*
I form the light and create darkness,
I make peace and create calamity;
I, the LORD, *do all these things.*"

ISAIAH 45:5–7

37

SOVEREIGN KING, HEAVENLY FATHER, EMMANUEL

I n today's passage Almighty God boldly proclaimed through the prophet Isaiah the truth that He is Lord, that He is *the* Lord, and that there is no one like Him. God is all-powerful, all-wise, and all-loving. He acts according to His sovereign and eternal plan of salvation, and He acts according to the good plans He has for you (Jeremiah 29:11). We need never doubt His resolve or His strength, His concern or His involvement, His grace or His goodness. Furthermore, God is in complete control of everything going on in this world.

In addition, God is our heavenly Father who loves giving good gifts to His children. One of those good gifts is His peace that we often feel when there is no other reason than His love for us. Jesus has also given us His Spirit to—among other things—live within us, guide us, give us wisdom, and help us understand Scripture.

May I suggest that, before your day gets going, you

ask God to go before you and to give you wisdom and courage throughout the day to be all He has called you to be? Your ever-present Lord wants you to build your life around Him, and He wants you to walk through each day with Him. The name *Emmanuel*, "God with us," is a solid fact and yet another reason we can know peace.

REFLECTION

What role does the Holy Spirit play in your life? What role does He want to play? What will you do to live with greater awareness that God is with you?

Behold what manner of love the Father has bestowed on us, that we should be called children of God!

1 JOHN 3:1

38

BEHOLD!

We owe our salvation to the love and grace of God—period. By sending His Son to die on the cross as the sacrificial Lamb serving as payment for our sin, God has saved us from eternal punishment for our sin, from eternal separation from Him. God has saved us not because of anything we've done. God saved us for His name's sake and definitely not because we deserve it.

This gracious and loving God, however, may sometimes allow you to enter a tight spot and difficult circumstances. But remember, whenever He guides you, He does so to be with you. And when God is near, you will undoubtedly know the peace you want, the peace you need. God also wants to be with you so you can know what He wants you to do. He gladly tells us in His Word, but He can also speak to our hearts. Have you ever stopped long enough to listen for His guiding voice? The Lord wants the best for you. That is why He wants you to be faithful and lean on Him. God loves you more than any mother or father has ever loved a son or daughter. Everything Almighty God does in your life—allows in your life—He does because He loves you. "Everything" includes the hard times of refinement and growth.

When was the last time you thanked God for His love, mercy, and grace? Take some time now. Praise Him for loving you with an everlasting and deeply personal love.

REFLECTION

In case you glossed over it, I'm going to encourage you again: Spend some time right now thanking God for His love, mercy, and grace. Praise Him for loving you with an everlasting and deeply personal love.

How beautiful upon the mountains
Are the feet of him who brings good news,
Who proclaims peace,
Who brings glad tidings of good things,
Who proclaims salvation,
Who says to Zion,
"Your God reigns!"

ISAIAH 52:7

39

PROCLAIMING PEACE

In this single verse, we find several aspects of God's good news that we can share in this darkened and lost world. If you have named Jesus your Savior and Lord, consider the good news you can proclaim: peace with God; glad tidings of grace, forgiveness, and eternity with God; salvation from the consequences of our sin because Jesus took on those consequences when He hung on the cross; and the peace and hope we find in the truth of God's sovereignty throughout all of history and around this entire globe. Now ask the Lord to recognize the people in your world who need to hear your proclamation of this very good news.

Or maybe you consider yourself one who needs to hear the good news. If so, know that the Lord—our good Shepherd—is calling you to Himself. He recognizes our lostness even when we don't. He longs to guide us out of harm's way and into the good things He has for us. And consider the love that fuels His calling: "God has sent His only begotten Son into the world, that we might live through Him" (1 John 4:9). So have you named Jesus your Lord? If not, what is keeping you from entering into a personal relationship with Him? Know that Jesus is waiting with open arms for you to come to Him. He wants to love you with His everlasting love; walk with you every day of your life; and fill you with His Spirit.

Whether you entered into a forever relationship with Jesus forty seconds ago, four years ago, or anywhere in between or longer, thank the good Lord for the gifts of His peace that passes all understanding and of His promise to never leave you nor forsake you. What could be better than that?

REFLECTION

The apostle Peter wrote, "Always be ready to give a defense to everyone who asks you a reason for the hope that is in you" (1 Peter 3:15). Are you ready and able to explain the source of your hope? Echoing the verse from Isaiah, are you ready to proclaim peace and "glad tidings of good things"? Practice now. Practice every week until sharing the gospel comes as easily as talking about your favorite vacation.

"For a mere moment I have forsaken you,
But with great mercies I will gather you.
With a little wrath I hid My face from you for a
    moment;
But with everlasting kindness I will have mercy
    on you,"
Says the LORD, your Redeemer. . . .
For the mountains shall depart
And the hills be removed,
But My kindness shall not depart from you,
Nor shall My covenant of peace be removed,"
Says the LORD, who has mercy on you.

ISAIAH 54:7–8, 10

40

GOD'S COVENANT OF PEACE

I f you have ever wondered about the Lord's love for you, read again His promises here. Note specifically the time frames He mentioned: "everlasting"; "shall not depart from you"; and "nor . . . be removed." Those words stand in sharp contrast to the love of a human being—or a golden retriever. We can easily lose the kinds of love the world offers us . . . except when the love being extended is redeemed love. What do I mean by that?

When we place our faith in Jesus and pledge to live with Him as our Lord, we are filled with the Holy Spirit who enables us to do things we can't do in our own power. The Spirit, for instance, enables us to love the hard to love, to love people when they're going through difficult times, to love when we get nothing in return, and to love simply because God commands us to love.

Loving others with Jesus' love doesn't mean that we won't get hurt along the way. We can know, however, that the pain God allows us to experience in this world is not for naught. God will use the hard times to refine, strengthen, and grow our faith. And in those hard times we can turn to the covenant promises of His Word, to His promises of "great mercies" and "everlasting kindness." And these promises bring hope and peace.

REFLECTION

Think about the hard times of your life. Then look at those experiences through the lens of Isaiah 54:7–8 and 10. What is the impact, if any, of this perspective? What encouragement, for instance, do you find? Finally, in what specific ways have you seen God *not* waste the pain in your life?

Seek the LORD while He may be found,
Call upon Him while He is near. . . .
"For My thoughts are not your thoughts,
Nor are your ways My ways," says the LORD.
"For as the heavens are higher than the earth,
So are My ways higher than your ways,
And My thoughts than your thoughts. . . .
"So shall My word be that goes forth from My
           mouth;
It shall not return to Me void,
But it shall accomplish what I please,
And it shall prosper in the thing for which I sent
           it."

ISAIAH 55:6, 8–9, 11

41

SEEKING THE LORD

Isaiah 55 opens with the Lord's call to come to Him, to come get water for their thirst and food for their hunger—and all "without money and without price" (v. 1). Our Lord invites us to come boldly into His presence to receive His counsel, confess our sins, make requests, and simply enjoy His company.

Then in verses 8–9 we find a reason to keep coming when we are disheartened, weighed down by our failure to understand what God is up to in our lives. Such lack of understanding may or may not happen frequently. However often we are bewildered and discouraged, our Lord asks us to trust Him. He invites us to choose to believe that He knows what He is doing even if we cannot comprehend at all His methods or His timing. The secret to living a life of faith that honors God is to trust in Him with all of our hearts (Proverbs 3:5).

In verse 11 we find yet another reason to trust the Lord. There He promises that His Word "shall not return to Me void, but it shall accomplish what I please." The context of this bold statement is God's comparing His

Word with rain that waters the earth and, as a result, brings forth flower and fruit (v. 10). What peace we can find in the bold statement that His Word "shall accomplish what I please"! After all, this bold assertion is a statement made by our ever-faithful promise-making and promise-keeping God!

God's Word never fails to achieve its aim. May we therefore embrace it, believe it, and build our lives on it.

REFLECTION

Consider why we human beings need to be invited by God Himself to seek Him and to call upon Him. What keeps you from answering that call—and what will you do to remove those obstacles to regularly spending time with Him? In other words, what will you do—how will you rearrange your routine—to make the reading and study of Scripture a priority in your life?

*Who is wise and understanding among you?
Let him show by good conduct that his works are
done in the meekness of wisdom. . . . The wisdom
that is from above is first pure, then peaceable,
gentle, willing to yield, full of mercy and good fruits,
without partiality and without hypocrisy. Now the
fruit of righteousness is sown in peace by those who
make peace.*

JAMES 3:13, 17–18

42

WISDOM FROM ABOVE

S ometimes defining a term—*divine wisdom*—is made easier by saying what that term is not, and James helped us do exactly that. The wisdom that the world offers is characterized by envy, self-seeking, confusion, and evil. Such human wisdom leads to arrogance and dissension. Perhaps the reliance on the wisdom of the world—and the very human choice to act according to our own cleverness—explains at least in part the amount of chaos, anger, and hatred in the world today.

So, in contrast, what kind of wisdom comes from God? James began his description by saying "the wisdom that is from above is first pure." This spiritual wisdom might be defined as "free from dust, dirt, or taint; free from harshness or roughness; containing nothing that does not properly belong." Imagine being guided by such wisdom! What an influence God's wisdom can have on our thoughts, words, and deeds; on doctrine and practice; in faith and in morality. We read that—always kept pure—godly wisdom is also peaceable, gentle, respectful of others, open to reason, willing to yield, merciful, bearing good fruit, compassionate, kind, and humble. Who comes to mind when you read this description? I agree: the Lord Jesus.

And the description continues. A person wise with the wisdom of heaven is authentic, the same person to all people, a speaker of the truth, merciful, helpful, genuine, a peacemaker, and one who has a servant heart. What a winsome witness to heavenly wisdom!

REFLECTION

Think of a wise person other than Jesus whom you know, a person who relies and has relied on heavenly wisdom as a compass and a map for life. Ideally, grab a cup of coffee with that person and talk about God-given wisdom—how, for instance, this person cultivates it, lives by it, and has been blessed by it.

"The Helper, the Holy Spirit, whom the Father will send in My name, He will teach you all things, and bring to your remembrance all things that I said to you. Peace I leave with you, My peace I give to you; not as the world gives do I give to you. Let not your heart be troubled, neither let it be afraid. You have heard Me say to you, 'I am going away and coming back to you.' If you loved Me, you would rejoice because I said, 'I am going to the Father,' for My Father is greater than I.

"And now I have told you before it comes, that when it does come to pass, you may believe."

JOHN 14:26–29

43

SURRENDERING TO PEACE

DIANE STRACK

Diane Strack is the wife and helpmate of Jay Strack, who is the president of Student Leadership University, and she is the founder of She Loves Out Loud, a global prayer movement for women. My wife and I have been blessed to call them friends for more than twenty-five years. Diane's life beautifully reflects God's mercy, grace, and love. In the past few years, she has had several heart procedures. She praises God for blessing her, protecting her, and giving her peace during one of those surgeries in particular.

I'd had more than a dozen stents, so when doctors suspected another blockage in my heart, I was in denial that this procedure could once again be necessary. So I asked—no, I insisted—that I would stay awake during the surgery. I wanted to see the damage for myself, a choice I will not make again. Staring at the giant screen while the doctor poked and prodded my arteries, I heard the cold reality of the spoken diagnosis. The words hit me hard, resulting not in the understanding I had hoped for but placing me in the steely grip of fear.

My first thought was *Be careful in there!* My second was *Stop it!* But the process was so overwhelming that I couldn't speak at all. Tears flowed down my cheeks as the arteries danced and rebelled against the probe. I can't even begin to describe the feeling of utter helplessness that tried to swallow me. Seeing the damage up close, I also knew that my life could easily have been over just minutes earlier, yet God had graciously given me another chance to live.

Silently, I cried, *Lord, meet me here. I need You here—and I need You now.* This heartfelt cry—this desperate demand—was inaudible to everyone except the Father. I tried to breathe as my fifteenth stent was threaded through my body and put in place. I know the doctors and nurses didn't hear it, but in that moment the Lord spoke to me in the commanding yet gentle voice that fathers sometimes use: "Present yourself to Me. I will do the rest."

Romans 12:1 came alive in me as, in submission to His command, I opened my palms: "Present your bodies a living sacrifice, holy, acceptable to God, which is your reasonable service." I learned in that moment that my presenting myself wholly and completely to God was His plan for me all along. He immediately released me from the grip of fear, and the dread that once held me captive drained into the cold, hard table beneath me. I remember smiling as a warm river of peace flooded my being.

While the doctors were working on my physical heart, the Lord was transforming my inner heart. His peace filled me and seemed to surround me. In full surrender to Him, I finally felt strong; in trusting Him, I was able to be confident about my future. I may have entered the doors to that dreaded cath lab without hope, but I walked out a woman transformed by God's peace—His gift to me, a gift for which I will always be grateful.

Presenting ourselves to God is an action for both the terrible and the ordinary. Doing so moves us beyond a life of merely adjusting to problems and circumstances. Instead, presenting ourselves to God takes us into an intimacy with the Savior so great that it cannot be explained but must be experienced. In those moments of surrender, the Lord will "smile on you . . . and give you his peace" (Numbers 6:25–26 NLT).

REFLECTION

Describe a moment when you presented yourself to God as "a living sacrifice, holy, acceptable to God, which is your reasonable service" (Romans 12:1). What impact did doing so have on you—body, mind, and soul? If you can't think of such a time, what is the significance of that realization? Also, why would such surrender be "your reasonable service"?

The L ORD spoke to Moses, saying, "Speak to Aaron and his sons, saying, 'This is the way you shall bless the Israelites. Say to them:

The L ORD bless you, and keep you [protect you,
 sustain you, and guard you];
The L ORD make His face shine upon you [with
 favor],
And be gracious to you [surrounding you with
 lovingkindness];
The L ORD lift up His countenance (face) upon
 you [with divine approval],
And give you peace [a tranquil heart and life].'

So Aaron and his sons shall put My name upon the children of Israel, and I will bless them."

NUMBERS 6:22–27 AMP

44

THE PRIESTLY
BLESSING OF PEACE

In the closing verses of Numbers 6 and on behalf of God Himself, Moses gave to Aaron the lovely and familiar blessing with which he and his sons were to bless the Lord's chosen people. And this blessing is as timely and relevant and life-giving today as it was millennia ago. Every heart may utter it, every day may be sanctified by it, and every night may be sealed by it.

As you incorporate this blessing into your life, let these words from the Lord draw you closer to the Lord and enrich your relationship with Him. God truly does want to bless His people with His grace, His favor, and His peace. He wants to bless us with the greatest blessing of all, and that is His very presence.

REFLECTION

When did you first hear this ancient blessing? What role, if any, has it played in your life? What role might it play in your life from this point on?

Now in Christ Jesus you who once were far off have been brought near by the blood of Christ.

For He Himself is our peace, who has made both one, and has broken down the middle wall of separation, having abolished in His flesh the enmity, that is, the law of commandments contained in ordinances, so as to create in Himself one new man from the two, thus making peace, and that He might reconcile them both to God in one body through the cross, thereby putting to death the enmity. And He came and preached peace to you who were afar off and to those who were near. For through Him we both have access by one Spirit to the Father.

EPHESIANS 2:13–18

45

PEACE WITH GOD, PEACE WITH OTHERS

L et's consider the message of the gospel in terms of peace.

First, the gospel is the simple and profound truth that "God so loved the world that He gave His only begotten Son, that whoever believes in Him should not perish but have everlasting life" (John 3:16). Jesus took the punishment for our sins when He died on the cross; He proved victorious over sin and death when He rose from the dead three days later; and He therefore made possible a relationship between holy God and sinful humanity. Jesus made possible peace between Creator and created; between Righteous and fallen; between Perfection and imperfection.

However, this good news—this gospel message—was not exclusively for God's chosen people, the Jews. God loved the world and therefore sent His Son, and Jesus died for "whoever believes in Him." To the utter shock of first-century Jewish believers, God revealed that Jesus also died for the Gentiles, for everyone who was not Jewish. The ancient enmity between Jew and Gentile was forever abolished. In addition to his explanation earlier, the apostle Paul said this: "by one Spirit we were all baptized into one body—whether Jews or Greeks, whether slaves or free" (1 Corinthians 12:13).

One more note about Paul's words. He wrote that "[Jesus] Himself is our peace." How can a person be peace? Something Jesus said offers a clue: "I am the way, the truth, and the life. No one comes to the Father except through Me" (John 14:6).

When a Jewish person believes on the Lord Jesus, their identity as a Christ-follower takes precedence over their identity as a Jew. Likewise, when a Gentile receives Jesus as Savior, that person's identity as a Christ-follower takes precedence over their identity as a Gentile. In other words, Jews and Gentiles were once divided; they were two separate people groups. But now their common commitment to Jesus unites the two groups into one. All who name Jesus as Lord and Savior are at peace with God and at peace with others who once believed differently.

REFLECTION

When, if ever, has a mutual love for Jesus been a bridge between you and someone who at one time was opposite to you in so many ways? What does such a uniting say to the watching world? On a more personal level, what identity of yours—if any—takes precedence over your identity as a Christ-follower? Ask the Holy Spirit to reveal the answer.

The LORD passed by [Elijah], and a great and strong wind tore into the mountains and broke the rocks in pieces before the LORD, but the LORD was not in the wind; and after the wind an earthquake, but the LORD was not in the earthquake; and after the earthquake a fire, but the LORD was not in the fire; and after the fire a still small voice.

1 KINGS 19:11–12

46

LISTENING FOR GOD

I magine hearing God's voice as easily as we recognize an earthquake or a fire! Thankfully, we can learn to hear and recognize His voice. We can develop a listening ear when we make time to sit in silence and wait upon Him to speak to us.

Maybe you make listening to God a regular part of your prayer time. Maybe—aware that you won't necessarily recognize His voice every time—you make it a spiritual discipline to wait in God's presence for Him to guide or encourage or convict you. If so, think about the last time you knew God's small, quiet voice had a word of wisdom, direction, or hope for you.

Be encouraged by Jeremiah 29:12–13: "You will call upon Me and go and pray to Me, and I will listen to you. And you will seek Me and find Me, when you search for Me with all your heart."

And act with confidence in the truth that God wants to interact with you throughout every day and share His wisdom, love, and peace with you. Learn to listen for His voice. Ask Him to help you develop a discerning spirit as well as a sensitive heart, and be prepared to obey Him.

REFLECTION

Why do you think God chooses a still small voice rather than the verbal equivalent to an earthquake or fire?

[Jesus'] disciples said to Him, "See, now You are speaking plainly, and using no figure of speech! Now we are sure that You know all things, and have no need that anyone should question You. By this we believe that You came forth from God."

JOHN 16:29–30

47

STRAIGHT TALK

Jesus asked His disciples, "Do you now believe?" Is He asking you the same question? Is Jesus wondering if He has finally done enough for you that you believe He is God and that you will name Him your Savior? And if you aren't convinced, what would it take?

Jesus' disciples appreciated His switch from "figurative language" to His "speaking plainly, and using no figure of speech!" We need to follow Jesus' example. We need to be able to clearly and straightforwardly explain what we believe: when He was crucified, Jesus paid the price for our sins so that we might have a personal relationship with Him now and throughout eternity. In addition, after Jesus' death and resurrection, He gave us His Spirit to teach, guide, comfort, convict, and even pray for us. Are you willing to rely on the Spirit and be bold about your faith? Jesus calls each of us, His followers, to share His love with our friends as well as with everyone else He puts in our path.

God calls each of us to be His witnesses to Him in this lost world. Who knows? Someone you talk to about your relationship with Jesus just may enter a saving relationship with Him because of your testimony. So let your light shine! When you do so, God can and will use you to let others see Christ in you.

REFLECTION

Think about the years of your life before you started following Jesus. Looking back, who did He place along your path to help you recognize your need for the Lord or to recognize that Jesus was the One who can take away the eternal consequences of your sin? If possible, contact that person or even a couple of them to let them know how much you appreciate how God used them in your life.

The same day at evening, being the first day of the week, when the doors were shut where the disciples were assembled, for fear of the Jews, Jesus came and stood in the midst, and said to them, "Peace be with you." When He had said this, He showed them His hands and His side. Then the disciples were glad when they saw the Lord.

So Jesus said to them again, "Peace to you! As the Father has sent Me, I also send you." And when He had said this, He breathed on them, and said to them, "Receive the Holy Spirit. If you forgive the sins of any, they are forgiven them; if you retain the sins of any, they are retained."

JOHN 20:19–23

48

OUR COMMISSION, THE SPIRIT'S POWER

When the resurrected Jesus spoke the words "Peace be with you" to His disciples, those words had more significance than they had ever had before. After all, Jesus Christ had made peace between holy God and sinful man by shedding His blood, dying on the cross, and rising from the tomb three days later. Those who are justified by faith have peace with God.

After pronouncing peace over His disciples, Jesus showed them the marks of His passion, by which peace with God had been obtained. They saw where the nails had pierced and the spear had wounded Him. When the disciples recognized Jesus, their hearts filled with joy at the realization that Jesus was truly the Lord. The events had unfolded exactly as He had said they would, and He had risen from the dead.

No wonder the risen Lord is the source of our Christian joy! The Father sent His Son into the world to save sinful human beings from an eternity of separation from perfectly holy Him. God's sending Jesus makes it possible for sinful men and women to enter into a relationship with God, and Jesus sends His followers out into the world to tell others about His invitation to salvation and relationship.

A final thought here: If the Word of God were not living and active by the power of the Spirit, it would have fallen into obscurity long ago. But it still rings with the truth that God is accomplishing its purpose, which is to lead people to Christ. That is our calling, and we should embrace it with joy and share the gospel with God's love.

REFLECTION

Maybe it's a trite condensation of the message today, but it expresses the same truth: When God calls us to do something, He empowers us to do that exact task through the Holy Spirit. When have you done what looked daunting, if not impossible, by the power of the Holy Spirit? What role can the Holy Spirit have as you respond to God's commission to share the gospel truth with the world?

"You, child, will be called the prophet of the Highest;
For you will go before the face of the Lord to prepare His ways,
To give knowledge of salvation to His people
By the remission of their sins,
Through the tender mercy of our God,
With which the Dayspring from on high has visited us;
To give light to those who sit in darkness and the shadow of death,
To guide our feet into the way of peace."

So the child grew and became strong in spirit, and was in the deserts till the day of his manifestation to Israel.

LUKE 1:76-80

49

DESIRING GOD'S PEACE

TRACEY MITCHELL

I have known author, speaker, and evangelist Tracey Mitchell for about fifteen years. We reconnect almost every year at the National Radio Broadcasting (NRB) Convention. I have seen her ministry grow as she sought the Lord's will, relied on the help of the Holy Spirit, and as a result made right decisions that led to new ways she served her Lord and Savior, Jesus Christ.

A few years ago, I was tempted to take a shortcut to success. It happened late one evening when I received a call from a West Coast talent agency. The person calling asked if I could meet with their representative in Dallas to discuss how the company might represent my work. Excited by the opportunity, I rearranged my schedule and drove to Texas. I wish I could tell you that I spent hours in prayer before leaving home, but I didn't. If I had been paying more attention to the inner nudge of the Holy Spirit, I would have never agreed to walk into that meeting. The truth is, sometimes we don't notice the enemy's trap until we are standing inside it.

After lunch with the agency members, I was escorted into a suite to meet with the vice president and several other VIPs. The small talk was complimentary, and the representatives offered a polished presentation and a financial package that was more lucrative than I could have imagined. It didn't merely involve thousands; it involved millions.

If I'm honest, the words they spoke were as enticing as the offer. They used phrases that my wounded heart longed to hear. After I listened to the proposal for a few hours, they pushed a gold pen into the palm of my hand. In what seemed like a cinematic moment, a man leaned forward and said, "All of this can be yours! All you have to do is sign with our agency." They smiled, and I nodded. After all, everything in that contract was exactly what I had spent decades working toward. As I reached for the deal, my heart sank, and my peace left. In a way that is hard to explain, I felt as though the oxygen had been suddenly sucked out of the room.

I stared at them, and they stared back. The man

motioned for me to take the paper, and I pulled my hand back. I couldn't explain my hesitation. In fact, I made myself nervous! They pushed the contract forward, and I felt the Holy Spirit pull me back. I had walked with God long enough to know what it feels like for Him to say, "Tracey, this isn't for you." Walking out of that meeting without a deal was one of the hardest things I've ever done. In fact, on the drive home, I cried bitter tears. It took me a while to find comfort in knowing that God would never ask me to walk away from something if He didn't have something more significant in my future.

As I look back at the business opportunity, I realize I could have quickly fallen into a trap so strong that I could never have pried my way free. God protected me by pulling back His peace.

I also learned that not everything that entices us away from God's perfect plan for us appears evil. Sometimes the trap is set in a way that seems neither good nor bad, but simply comfortable.

REFLECTION

What is your major takeaway from Tracey's story? Why? To what current situation in your life, if any, does it apply or might it be helpful? Explain.

Rejoice in the Lord always. Again I will say, rejoice! Let your gentleness be known to all men. The Lord is at hand. Be anxious for nothing, but in everything by prayer and supplication, with thanksgiving, let your requests be made known to God; and the peace of God, which surpasses all understanding, will guard your hearts and minds through Christ Jesus.

PHILIPPIANS 4:4–7

50

ON DUTY

JAY STRACK

I have known Jay Strack for more than thirty years, and I've seen his ministry—Student Leadership University—touch the lives of thousands of teenagers, often with the simple teaching that God is a God of peace who cares deeply for each and every one of us.

For several decades, I have relied on the apostle Paul's instruction in Philippians 4:4: "Rejoice in the Lord always." In this chapter, Paul focused on the duty, the discipline, and the delight of rejoicing in the Lord of all. The command applies to all circumstances, even past sin that still tries to drag us into depression and rob us of hope. For Paul, this discipline required great effort, for he was reminded daily of his murderous past of persecuting the very Christians he now loved and cared for. In addition, Paul constantly faced the threat of suffering and imprisonment. Even so, in that same verse, Paul repeated, "Again I will say, rejoice!" as though he wanted to emphasize further that no situation or challenge was exempt. Such tenacity in rejoicing was a hallmark of Paul's life, just as it must be in every believer's.

An anonymous author wrote, "Peace is the smile of God in the soul of a believer." Perhaps Paul thought something similar as he followed up the command to rejoice with "Let your gentleness be known to all men" (v. 5). Surely one cannot exist without the other. To rejoice is to show peace to others. So important is the peace of God that Paul opened every one of his epistles with a blessing of peace.

Optimism rather than pessimism is possible, Paul explained, when you "let your requests be made known to God" (v. 6). Paul understood the power of asking, believing, and having gratitude. On those days when God is the only One who can remove the barrier or the only One still standing with you, "let your requests be made known to [Him]."

The peace of God originates in God Himself, and this peace "surpasses all understanding." At the same time, it is the great gift that "will guard your hearts and minds through Christ Jesus" (v. 7). Digging into the historical word picture of this passage, I can imagine that the people Paul addressed in that day were used to seeing

Roman centurions standing guard in the most famous legions of armies in the known world. They understood immediately the power of this peace of God to protect, defend, guard, watch, and stand in front of the enemy.

In days of cultural change, division, conflict, betrayals, dishonesty, disappointments—and the list goes on—we can claim the peace of God as our protection. I'll explain by first noting that I have always been moved by the sight of the uniformed guard at the Tomb of the Unknown Soldier at Arlington Cemetery. On the side of the marble sarcophagus are sculpted three Greek figures representing peace, victory, and valor. The back of the tomb is inscribed with the phrase "Here rests in honored glory an American soldier known but to God." The tomb is guarded 24/7, 365 days a year, in any and all weather conditions. These military guards offer us a beautiful picture of the peace of God that guards our hearts and minds. All conditions; all circumstances; all the time. He knows your name.

REFLECTION

Review today's opening passage, Philippians 4:4–7. To which charge does obedience come most easily? Which charge do you struggle most to obey? Why? And what steps can you take toward greater obedience? After all, God's commands are for our good.

Let Your tender mercies come to me, that I may
live;
For Your law is my delight.
Let the proud be ashamed,
For they treated me wrongfully with falsehood;
But I will meditate on Your precepts.

PSALM 119:77–78

51

GOD'S COMMANDMENTS ARE FOR YOU

Despite how some of them sound to us, all of God's commandments are for our benefit, for He loves to bless us with life and peace. Whenever we turn away from God's Word, we are turning away from both life and peace.

Even though we turn away from Him, our gracious God still wants to be both guiding our steps by His Spirit and protecting us from the Evil One. And God will always be like that. In fact, God is immutable, meaning He never changes. He operates on eternal unchanging principles, and that's why we can build our lives on His promises.

As we seek the Lord and ask for His help in grasping His truth and building our lives on it, we find that God's truth facilitates our faithfulness to our calling.

Furthermore, by the power of the Holy Spirit, the Lord will supply all the biblical insight and knowledge we will ever need through the Holy Spirit. Still, it is wise to memorize certain verses of Scripture to guide and protect us as we seek to serve Jesus. In my life, every verse that I memorize and hide in my heart becomes a shield for battle and a sword of truth for my testimony.

As I have grown older, my relationship with the Lord has become the most important thing. I also deeply appreciate the peace that I cannot explain, a peace that I have whatever life's circumstances.

Most important, I appreciate the peace that I have with my Savior.

REFLECTION

Why do you—and all of us do this—turn away from commands that are for your good and that lead to life and peace? What steps can you take toward greater obedience? After all, God's commands are for our good.

Bless the LORD, O my soul;
And all that is within me, bless His holy name!
Bless the LORD, O my soul,
And forget not all His benefits:
Who forgives all your iniquities,
Who heals all your diseases,
Who redeems your life from destruction,
Who crowns you with lovingkindness and
        tender mercies . . .
For as the heavens are high above the earth,
So great is His mercy toward those who fear
        Him;
As far as the east is from the west,
So far has He removed our transgressions from
        us.

PSALM 103:1–4, 11–12

52

FORGIVENESS IS A WONDERFUL THING

Scripture plainly tells us that God loves us just the way we are. He wants every part of us—body, soul, and spirit—to grow close to Him and enter into a joyful relationship with Him. He seeks worshipers who will gladly give everything they are to Him. Jesus paid the ultimate sacrifice so that the gateway to God would be open and we can have a personal relationship with the Father. When God looks down on us, He sees us as pure, without sin, and perfect all because of Jesus. This gift is given to us who accept Jesus as our personal Lord and Savior, and we are blessed beyond our imagination. Therefore, let each day be filled with God's presence as we walk through life hand in hand with our Lord and Savior. God has a plan for us. Do not let your life miss anything God has planned for you. If you have not accepted His gift, do so today and let His light shine through you. With God's forgiveness comes the beautiful reward of peace.

REFLECTION

Let today be the first day of the rest of your life. You are a child of the King. God is waiting patiently to guide and direct your life for His glory and your benefit.

ACKNOWLEDGMENTS

I want to give a heartfelt thank-you to the twenty people who contributed their stories of peace through difficult situations. Each of you shared how God helped you find peace and made this book meaningful to the reader. God cares for us, and your contribution made that abundantly clear in many different situations presented in the book.

Roland Colson
Marsha Countryman
Hank Hanegraaff
O. S. Hawkins
Joey Hickman
Jimmy Houston
Dr. Johnny Hunt
Brian Jorgenson
Dr. James Law
Scott Lehman
Anne Graham Lotz
Tracey Mitchell
Regina Prude
Bruce Pulver
Beth Ryan
Diane Strack
Jay Strack
Steve Sturges
Chuck Wallington
Dr. Don Wilton

LET GOD DRAW YOU NEAR

JACK COUNTRYMAN

THE POWER OF
HOPE

100 DEVOTIONS
to Build
Your Faith

ISBN 978-1-4002-2496-8

World headlines and our personal struggles can leave us feeling weary and anxious. But life's questions and our emotions are not new to God. If you are feeling exhausted, worried, or lonely or are facing difficulties, *The Power of Hope* by Jack Countryman offers a beautiful reminder that the same God who comforted and blessed the people of the Bible can offer you transformation and peace today.

Available at
bookstores everywhere!

COUNTRYMAN®
An Imprint of Thomas Nelson Publishers

THOMAS NELSON®
Since 1798
thomasnelson.com

LOVING GOD: OUR HIGHEST PRIORITY

As the deer pants for the water brooks,
So pants my soul for You, O God.
My soul thirsts for God, for the living God.
When shall I come and appear before God? . . .
Why are you cast down, O my soul?
And why are you disquieted within me?
Hope in God, for I shall yet praise Him
For the help of His countenance.
PSALM 42:1-2, 5

The Psalmist

W hat does God want most from us? He wants us to love Him. He created us to be in intimate relationship with Him. He made us to thirst for Him with the same intensity we have when, parched and dry, we seek water for our physical thirst.

Sometimes—like this psalmist—we don't even know why we feel dry, why we feel discouraged or sad. In those times we need to *choose* to put our hope in God, to draw on His strength, and to receive the grace He has for us. May we also remember that God loves us with an everlasting love, and He truly wants the best for us. He longs for us to go to Him regularly with our hearts open to receive His love, mercy, and grace.

When your relationship with God is your highest priority, you will know divine strength and unshakable hope.

HONORING OUR GOD

Blessed are You, LORD God of Israel,
our Father, forever and ever.
Yours, O LORD, is the greatness,
The power and the glory,
The victory and the majesty. . . .
In Your hand is power and might;
In Your hand it is to make great
And to give strength to all.
I CHRONICLES 29:10-12

David

King David wanted to build a house for his great, powerful, glorious God, but the Lord gave that privilege to David's son Solomon.

To honor God and help Solomon succeed, David gave his personal fortune—about 113 tons of gold and 214 tons of silver—to the building project. Then David invited the people to join him. They, too, gave willingly and generously: 188 tons of gold, 377 tons of silver, 679 tons of bronze, 3,775 tons of iron, and precious jewels (1 Chronicles 28–29 MSG). No wonder David responded with a song of praise!

The people had been generous. Perhaps they understood what we need to understand and remember: everything we have comes from God. We give nothing to God that He, our good Father, has not first given to us. Who wouldn't praise such a God?

Like the Israelites, may we worship God by joyfully, generously giving to His work in this world.

3

THE GREATEST POWER: LOVE

Love suffers long and is kind; love does not envy;
love does not parade itself, is not puffed up; does
not behave rudely, does not seek its own, is not
provoked, thinks no evil; does not rejoice in iniquity,
but rejoices in the truth; bears all things, believes
all things, hopes all things, endures all things.

Love never fails. . . . Now abide faith, hope, love,
these three; but the greatest of these is love.
I CORINTHIANS 13:4-8, 13

Paul

T he author of these well-known 1 Corinthians 13 verses is the apostle Paul. On a murderous mission to destroy Jesus-followers, Paul himself became a follower (Acts 9). He had witnessed Stephen's stoning, "made havoc of the church" (Acts 8:3), and then set off to Damascus to continue his persecution of believers—yet later he wrote 1 Corinthians 13. Apparently those Jesus-followers Paul had once persecuted taught him a lot about Christian love.

God *is* love. The gift of His Son to die on the cross for our sins reveals His love. When we pray and He says, "Not yet," we can trust in His love. When people disappoint and tragedies occur, we can trust in His love. When we face difficult decisions, we can depend on His guiding love. When God's love is our dwelling place, we live with hope, finding strength for the day and abundant love to share.

20

HOPING IN OUR SOVEREIGN GOD

Esther was taken to King Ahasuerus, into his royal palace, in the tenth month, which is the month of Tebeth, in the seventh year of his reign. The king loved Esther more than all the other women, and she obtained grace and favor in his sight more than all the virgins; so he set the royal crown upon her head and made her queen.

ESTHER 2:16–17

Esther

God often demonstrates His grace to His children by giving us not only unexpected blessings but also unexpected power or influence. Whenever the latter happens, it is no accident. That power or influence is the plan of our sovereign God.

It was, for instance, His sovereign hand that placed Esther on the throne in Persia, a position that gave Esther an opportunity to live out in a bold way the strength she found when she placed her hope in God. Queen Esther risked her life by going—uninvited—before the king to arrange a time when she could ask him to prevent the genocide of her Jewish people. God showed her grace and favor when He prompted the king to show her grace and favor. And as He did for Esther, God will do for you whenever you boldly live out your hope in your sovereign God.

ABOUT THE AUTHOR

Jack Countryman is the founder of JCountryman gift books, a division of Thomas Nelson, and is the recipient of the Evangelical Christian Publishers Association's Jordan Lifetime Achievement Award. Over the past thirty years, he has developed best-selling gift books such as *God's Promises® for Your Every Need*, *God's Promises® for Men*, *God's Promises® for Women*, *God Listens*, and *The Red Letter Words of Jesus*. Countryman's books have sold more than 27 million units. His graduation books alone have sold more than 1.6 million units.